CONVERSATIONS WORTH HAVING

Gospel Wisdom for College Students

This book is dedicated to—
Pastor David Prince
and
Pastor Jeremy Haskins—
men who embody gospel wisdom
for the church.

CONTENTS

Preface   5

Gospel Roots
  Not the Center   7
  How to be More Spiritual   10
  Just Be Yourself   14
  Not Radical Enough   18
  Your Biggest Problem   21
  Living Free   25
  God Can Do Whatever He Wants   28
  Christian = Witness   31

Gospel Community
  Why John Piper Can't be Your Mentor   34
  Consuming the Church   37
  Ordinary Folks You Can't Live Without   41
  Going to Church is Too Safe   44
  How to Grow Spiritually   47

Gospel Living
  The Idol of Convenience   50
  Feeling Good   53
  Staying Safe   56
  Am I Allowed?   59
  Godly Masculinity?   63
  Time Management   66

Never Again!   69
A Plea for Thicker Skin   72
Liberating Prayer   76
How to Find the Will of God   80
Don't be Wimpy   83
The Majesty of Mundane   86
Why G-Rated Is Dangerous   90
Why Are You So Distracted?   93

Gospel Relationships
Disney Love vs. Crucified Love   96
Dating Advice   99
More Dating Advice   104
Real Dating Tips for Real Men   108

Appendix
Recommended Reading   112

Preface

This book is something of an accident. What I mean is that I never really intended to write a book. Over the course of my ten years in college ministry, I began to notice that I was having the same types of conversations with students over and over, semester after semester. You know, the kinds of things college students obsess over: dating, marriage, missions, work, knowing God's will, dating, marriage, choosing a career, campus ministries, dating, and marriage. So, naturally, as the same themes played on repeat continually, I began to codify a catalogue of college ministry talking points. And as a father of five and someone who works with middle school and high school students, I also began to wonder if this material would be helpful for parents as they prepare their children for the next stage of life. Could we root out some of these issues by intentionally having these conversations before college? I think we can.

So how should you use this book? The answer to this question is simple: Anyway you would like. The chapters are short enough to be placed conveniently on coffee tables or in restroom libraries. I wrote 31 chapters so that you could use it as a once-a-day devotional for a month. The themes are particularly relevant for high school age through college/graduate school. Disciplers might use this book to launch into important discipleship topics with those they are training. I would hope that campus ministers would find it helpful and stimulating. Parents may want to use it as a guide for conversations or family devotions as they prepare their young adults for the next stage in life. Churches may want to give it away to graduates.

However it's used, I pray that it would serve to edify the church of the Lord Jesus Christ as the all-wise God sees fit.

Not the Center

I know what they've always told you. College is a time for you to have fun. These four (or six or eight) years need to be about you. Enjoy them. You'll never get this time back. In fact, I know that this is the message you've likely heard your whole life. There's a reason they didn't keep score in your Upward basketball games. You shouldn't ever have to experience losing. You're a winner! There's a reason you always got a trophy, no matter how well you played. You need to feel good about yourself. Life is really about you and your happiness. At least, that's what they've always told you. But what if all that was a lie?

Jesus came into the world preaching a radically different message than the one described above. He called anyone who wished to follow him to "deny himself and take up his cross daily" (Luke 9:23).[1] Philippians 2:6-8 describes how he actually demonstrated this lifestyle he calls us to live: "Though he was in the form of God, [he] did not count equality with God a thing to be grasped, but made himself nothing, taking the form of a servant, being born in the likeness of men. And being found in human form, he humbled himself by becoming obedient to the point of

---

[1] All Scripture quotations come from the English Standard Version.

death, even death on a cross." Jesus, the Son of God, became a human being and died in order to bring salvation to the world.

Many of you reading this book are familiar with this message. Maybe you've even read these very passages. But there's a problem. There's a tendency to hear even this message about Christ as if it's just another chapter in the great story about us. We often want to co-opt Jesus into our pre-existing lives. He becomes the fulfillment of all our desires, the One who makes all our dreams come true. In this story that we write, Jesus died and was raised primarily to bring us happiness-as-we-define-it. So our reasoning often sounds a lot like this: "Will my unbelieving boyfriend or girlfriend make me happy? Well then, of course God wants me to date him or her!" "Does church membership feel like a drag? God certainly wouldn't want me to do anything that doesn't feel right!" "Do I struggle with same-sex attraction? God would never ask me to deny the way I feel!" According to this mentality, there is one main question to ask when it comes to my decision-making as a Christian: Is this what I want to do?

But what if God is in the business of calling us to do things that don't feel right, at least not initially? What if he's really a King to be obeyed rather than a genie to fulfill our wishes? Check out the rest of the passage from Philippians: "Therefore God has highly exalted him and bestowed on him the name that is above every name, so that at the name of Jesus every knee should bow, in heaven and on earth, and every tongue confess that Jesus Christ is Lord, to the glory of God the Father" (Phil. 2:9-11). Why did Jesus humble himself and die? For the glory of God the Father. Let that sink in. Jesus did what he did in order to bring glory to the God of the universe. Salvation is about God before it is about us. Jesus is not a part of our story. We get to be a part of his story. He is the central reality of the universe.

This perspective changes everything. "He died for all, that those who live might no longer live for themselves but for him who for their sake died and was raised" (2 Cor. 5:15). Jesus died on the cross to pay for the sins of the world. He rose from the dead to win his people eternal life with him in his kingdom. We enter into this salvation by repenting of our sins and trusting in him. From that moment on, life is no longer about us. Before Christ, the dominating question in our lives is: "What do I want to do? What will give me the most pleasure now?" Now, after receiving the salvation Christ won for us, the dominating question of our lives has radically changed: "What is his will? What will bring him the most glory and pleasure?" We find our joy in his glory. Every decision is now based upon a different question: Will this magnify Christ?

College and the rest of your life is a time for you to glorify God by crucifying your desires and asking him to replace those desires with his desires. Jesus is calling his followers to wad up our plans and throw them away. He writes the script for our lives. Any message that minimizes this reality is a lie. If you are in Christ, your time, your resources, and your life don't really belong to you anymore. It all belongs to God. In fact, you belong to God. You will never experience true and lasting joy, joy-as-God-defines-it, until you realize that Christ is the center and begin living in light of that reality.

How to be More Spiritual

"I just want to be led by the Spirit." Now that's a desire we can all get behind. What Christian doesn't want to be completely given over to the influence of the Holy Spirit? To have God the Spirit leading our lives should obviously be our goal. But why do I cringe every time I hear someone say something like this? Why do I get the feeling that when most people express such sentiments they are not meaning what the Bible means when it speaks to the Spirit-led life? There are three common errors that young Christians often make in regards to the Holy Spirit's involvement in the world.

The Spirit isn't opposed to doctrine, because he authored doctrine. There is a real tendency today to make a distinction between what is "spiritual" and what is "doctrinal." The mentality goes like this: When the Spirit is leading, we don't really need all that doctrine stuff. In fact, to emphasize doctrine might even quench the power of the Spirit. If we are really Spirit-led, the thinking goes, then we will put more emphasis on "spiritual" things like healing and other miracles and leave that doctrine stuff alone. Doctrine just causes arguments and is an intellectual substitute for real-life Christianity. If you're a real Christian, it will be reflected in a Spirit-led life, not a doctrinal commitment.

I want to be careful here, because I believe that a real error is being targeted. However, the solution being given is an equal error. The problem is that there really are Christians in our churches who emphasize doctrine while deemphasizing the connection between doctrine and the way they lead their lives. In fact, many young Christians communicate disillusionment over the fake kind of Christians they grew up around, people who showed up and checked the right doctrinal boxes while living immoral lives. This really is a problem, but the solution is not to rid the church of doctrine. The solution is to teach doctrine the same way the New Testament teaches it. Paul shows us the connection between doctrine and life in his letter to Titus.

In Tit. 2:1 Paul exhorts young Titus to "teach what accords with sound (or healthy) doctrine." How do you do this? The next nine verses spell it out, and these verses are all about life change. Doctrine in this context can be defined as teaching about Christ that is truthful. Believers can "adorn the doctrine of God our Savior" by living holy lives that are consistent with healthy doctrine, lives that are self-controlled (v. 2, 5, 11) and submissive (v. 5, 9, 3:1). In fact, the entire New Testament is concerned with two things when it comes to doctrine: 1) Is it true? Does it faithfully bear witness to Christ and the grace of the gospel? 2) Does it change lives? If the answer to either one of these questions is no, then we're missing the point of doctrine.

But under no circumstances can we dismiss doctrine as something unnecessary or unwanted within the church. We get our doctrine from the Bible, and let's not forget how we got the Bible: "For no prophecy was ever produced by the will of man, but men spoke from God as they were carried along by the Holy Spirit" (2 Pet. 1:21). The Spirit inspired the Bible from which we teach doctrine. True doctrine is his doctrine.

It is important that we teach things that are consistent with God's nature and ways. If what we teach is not true, we're a hopeless people and true heart change is impossible.

The Spirit must be separated clearly from one's emotional life. Just because you are a Christian doesn't mean that everything you want to do from this point on is in line with the Spirit's will. In other words you can't contradict the clear teachings of Scripture by appealing to how the Spirit is leading you. This may seem obvious, but I hear it often. We are all in danger of reducing the Spirit to a force that we can manipulate to get our way. We must remember that the Spirit is not some kind of Jedi force. He's the sovereign God of the universe. And if we want to know what he thinks, he's graciously told us in the Scriptures he inspired.

The Spirit is never divorced from Christ. A lot of emphasis gets put on healing and miraculous signs these days. It is not uncommon in my city to have complete strangers walk up in coffee shops and ask to pray for a specific bodily ailment that they claim God told them you have. They call these outings "treasure hunts." This practice indicates confusion about our central mission in the world today. We are not called to go out to heal bodily ailments. We are called to "make disciples of all nations" (Matt. 28:19). Obviously, we are never to ignore the injustices and suffering around us. Caring for those who are hurting is mandated by the very gospel we declare. But our ultimate goal is to "proclaim the excellencies of him who called you out of darkness into his marvelous light" (1 Pet. 2:9). We're not trying to temporarily heal people who are dying. Instead, we are offering everyone who repents and believes access into an eternal existence under the rule of Christ where suffering and injustice will be abolished forever. This mission is the Spirit's mission. Jesus said concerning the ministry of the Spirit, "When the Spirit of truth comes, he will guide you into all the truth, for he will not speak on his own authority, but whatever he hears he will speak, and he will declare to you the things that are to come. He will glorify me, for he will take what is mine and declare it to you" (John 16:13-14). To be Spirit-led is to be Christ-centered. If you are following Christ faithfully, it's because the Spirit is leading you to do so. If Christ isn't the point of your life and ministry, you're not Spirit-led. If you emphasize the Spirit more than you emphasize Christ, then you are actually ignoring the Spirit, for he came to point us to Christ. How do you know if you are Spirit-led? Are you growing in the gospel of Christ? Are you proclaiming the good news of salvation found in Christ? That's the Spirit-led life.

Not Radical Enough

The call to follow Jesus is a radical call. Our love and commitment to him must exceed our love and commitment to anyone else, including our own families (Matt. 10:34-39). Our entire lives must be given over to him (Luke 9:23-27). Dietrich Bonhoeffer, who was martyred under the orders of Adolf Hitler, stated the call like this: "When Christ calls a man, he bids him come and die." Jim Elliot, a missionary who was martyred by an indigenous tribe in Equador, had his own way of stating the call: "He is no fool who gives what he cannot keep to gain what he cannot lose." Throughout church history God has graciously raised up men like Bonhoeffer and Elliot to not only remind the church of this call with their writings, but also to display this call with the sacrifice of their very lives. In our generation, I am grateful for recent books which remind modern-day believers that Christ's demands haven't changed. Even in the West, to believe in Christ costs us everything. Americans don't get a Christianity-made-easy. God doesn't allow us to formulate a version of following Christ that never butts heads with the American Dream.

Numbers 6 introduces us to some pretty radical folks. The Nazirites were normal Israelites who voluntarily chose to sacrifice by taking a vow to the Lord. They functioned among God's people as living, breathing illustrations of holiness. Throughout the length of their vow, they couldn't drink wine or eat anything from the vine (6:3-4), cut their hair (6:5), or go near dead bodies, not even those from their own family (6:6-8). These people would have been considered the most radical in their society. They were the Bonhoeffers and Elliots of ancient Israel. Everyone in Israel would have looked to them as examples of the life lived for God. And yet, Numbers 6 gives us the unmistakable impression that these holy people weren't radical enough. After their vow was complete, the Nazirite was still not allowed to enter the tabernacle, where God's presence dwelt (6:13). The Nazirite still needed atonement for his or her sins and was required to make several sacrifices toward that end (6:14-18).

The Nazirites show us that radical living is never enough. No matter how radically we try to live, we are still sinners in need of atonement. There has only ever been one man whose level of radical devotion was good enough to enter into the presence of God. The writer of Hebrews explains, "But when Christ appeared as a high priest of the good things that have come, then through the greater and more perfect tent (not made with hands, that is, not of this creation) he entered once for all into the holy places, not by means of the blood of goats and calves but by means of his own blood, thus securing an eternal redemption" (9:11-12). Jesus could enter the holy places (the presence of God) because Jesus was without sin. He's the only man who completely loved God with his whole heart and loved his neighbor as himself. He's the only human being in history whose sinless devotion was radical enough.

So when we read the radical demands that the gospel makes on our lives, we must never make the mistake of thinking that living radically provides the way to acceptance by God. Salvation can never be earned by our radical living. Like the Nazirites, our only hope is the provision of sacrificial atonement that Jesus made on our behalf. As Jesus calls us to take up our crosses and follow him, we must remember that, in the very moment he is uttering those words in Luke's gospel, he himself is on his way to take up his own cross to die as a substitute for the sins of the world. The call to follow Christ is a radical call, but it's not our ability to be radical that's the point. Christ demands radical lives, because radical lives display the glory of the gospel. When we live in contrast to the world, we display a gospel worth believing in, a Savior worth following. But remember this: his love always precedes ours, and his devotion to us is always prior to our devotion to him. We can only die to ourselves, because he has first died and been raised to life again. The radical life is made possible by his radical sacrifice. It's the fruit of what he has already accomplished.

I think this perspective is vital for you as you seek to follow Christ as a college student or young adult. At this point in your life, you want your life to count for something. You are dreaming about accomplishing huge things for God. I pray that you will always pursue this. However, my fear is that, in dreaming big, you might shift your focus away from Christ and toward living a radical life. It's a subtle shift and will be very hard to see. The radical life must never become an end in itself. Even worse, it must never become a means toward self-glorification. Our lives are radical because our Lord is radical. As we seek to follow him, let's make sure he's the focus. Let's make sure we're doing everything we do for his glory and not our own.

Your Biggest Problem

Your circumstances are never a hindrance to your living of a godly life. Your situation is never the determiner of your state of mind. We love to think that the secret to our happiness, to our ability to live for God, lies in something that we lack "out there." If I only had more money, or a better job, or better roommates, or a boyfriend/girlfriend, or a husband/wife, *then* I could live up to my potential. *Then* I could do what God calls me to do. This mindset paralyzes us—enslaving us to circumstances beyond our control. It also completely takes the focus off of what really hinders us from living for God

Consider the apostle Paul. Have you ever read the biblical descriptions of what he went through as an apostle of Christ? If you have not, take a moment to read 2 Cor. 11:23-33. The Christian life is not easy, and the more committed you are to Christ and the gospel, the more difficulties you are going to face. Contrary to best-selling authors, God never promises "your best life now." All of the promises of Scripture about the best life are future-oriented promises. As long as our world and our hearts are tainted by sin, we should expect trouble. We must come to grips with the truth that our circumstances are never going to be ideal in this life. The conditions are never going to be good enough for your growth in godliness. There will always be elements in your life that seem out of control. You will likely spend the majority of your life feeling like you are falling behind, frantically trying to keep five plates spinning at one time. If you continue to put off the changes you need to make until your situation improves, you will never change. You will live your life enslaved to circumstances that you can't control.

Believe it or not, my intention here is not to depress you. The good news is coming. I want to offer you a gospel-shaped way to look at your circumstances, and I believe this new perspective has the power to revolutionize your life. If God is completely sovereign over all the circumstances of your life and he wills only your ultimate good, which is what Romans 8:28-30 is definitely telling us, might we conclude that your circumstances are not hindrances but actually opportunities for your growth in godliness? What if God is custom-making your life situation to provide you with a context that will maximize your potential to grow into Christ's likeness? So let's assume you hate traffic jams, but you seem to get involved in traffic congestion more than you think is necessary. Could God not be using these trials to provide a context in which to glorify him by allowing the Spirit to form patience and self-control within your heart? 2 Peter 1:3 reminds us that we have everything we need to live a life of godliness at any given moment: "His divine power has granted to us all things that pertain to life and godliness, through the knowledge of him who called us to his own glory and excellence."

Paul, that same apostle who lists his hardships in 2 Cor. 11:23-33, also models this gospel-centered mindset for us in Phil. 4:11-13: "Not that I am speaking of being in need, for I have learned in whatever situation I am to be content. I know how to be brought low, and I know how to abound. In any and every circumstance, I have learned the secret of facing plenty and hunger, abundance and need. I can do all things through him who strengthens me." It may surprise you that that last verse does not pertain to success on the athletic field. Paul is writing about his sufferings—his unpleasant circumstances. He says he has learned the secret of maintaining joy in the midst of it all. How? He is now interpreting his circumstances through the lens of the gospel. Jesus and his crucifixion now provide the model through which we are to understand all of life (Phil. 2:5-11). Jesus shows us that suffering leads to glory (Phil. 3:10-11). Our present circumstances are not the end of the story. The sin of this world will not have the final word. Jesus has defeated sin, suffering, and death through his crucifixion and resurrection. The victory now belongs to us—his followers! Certainly, we can now triumphantly exclaim, "I can do all things through him who strengthens me!"

Just Be Yourself

     .

"But I was born this way." Everyone's heard it. If you're like me, you've probably spoken it, or at least thought something like it. Perhaps it begins as you reflect on a particular sin or character flaw. Frustration easily sets in at the realization that you keep doing the same thing over and over again. In utter exasperation you begin to question if it's even possible to live obediently. "Perhaps I can't really help how I am," you begin to think. "Perhaps I'm just wired to fail in this area for the rest of my life." Cultural trends certainly feed this attitude. The homosexual cultural agenda has us asking questions like: Can we really blame people for their sexual orientation? Can people really help who they are attracted to? Why don't we just encourage people to be who they are, to live according to their own desires?

There's actually a hint of truth to these thoughts: God does want his people to be who they are. But God doesn't want you to be who you are as a fallen created being. He wants your life to be consistent with what he has recreated you to be in Christ. He doesn't want you to be who you were born to be; he wants you to be who you were reborn to be. If you are a Christian, a new creation (2 Cor. 5:17), then be yourself! Live in a manner that's consistent with who you really are! But here's the game-changing truth: You're not who you used to be. As a new creation, you've been born again to a whole new way of God-ward living. The old you lies dead on the very same cross where Jesus died. By virtue of your faith in Jesus, your identity is now found exclusively in him. God will never consider you outside of Christ again. Everything that belongs to Jesus now belongs to you. His righteousness, his inheritance, his atoning work—all yours! So if God never considers you apart from Jesus, should you? No! Being yourself as a Christian means that you now exist in the realm of the Spirit. You now belong to the Kingdom of Christ. You are dead to sin and alive to God. You are no longer a slave to sin. The power of Christ's resurrection now courses through your veins. "You must consider yourselves dead to sin and alive to God in Christ Jesus" (Rom. 6:11). Be who you were re-born to be!

So many of our sin struggles as Christians are tied to the fact that we forget who we really are in Christ. Think about it. If I believe that I'm enslaved to sin, is there any hope for real change? Will I really do the hard work of killing sin through the gospel if I believe it's not going to make a difference? The identity we assign ourselves powerfully shapes every move we make. Identity shapes everything, and we have a new identity as sons of God. So, next time you are struggling with a specific sin, it's a good idea to begin here. Ask yourself how you may be viewing yourself apart from Christ. Are you finding your identity in him or are you still trying to build an identity of your own, apart from him? Are you identifying yourself with Adam by virtue of creation or with Christ by virtue of re-creation?

Below are some practical tips that might help you to keep your focus where it needs to be. How do we practically remember that our identity is to be found only in Christ?

1. Seek to know God.

John Calvin once said, "Without knowledge of self there is no knowledge of God....Without knowledge of God there is no knowledge of self."[2] To know God rightly enables the sinful man or woman to know himself rightly. How could we exalt ourselves proudly when we are walking in intimate communion with the Triune God in all of his majesty? As we meditate on God's nature it reminds us of our smallness. As we meditate on God's holiness it reminds us of our sinfulness. We need these reminders.

2. Meditate on the Gospel.

Once we remember who we are in light of who God is, we must remember what God has done in Christ to bring us to him. The gospel is good news because it reminds us that no matter how bad we are God still loves us. In fact, he loves us enough to send his own Son to die for our sins so that we might be reconciled to God through faith. We need to believe this every single day of our lives. To move away from the gospel is to move into identity confusion. The gospel allows us to rest in Christ, since we no longer have to try to compensate for our failures by our own efforts. We are able to admit that we don't stack up to God's standard. We can't fix this problem, but Christ already has. He lived the perfect life that we could never live. He paid the insurmountable debt that we owed. He rose from the dead to defeat our greatest enemy, death. We gain from his reward by grace alone.

---

[2] John Calvin, *Institutes of the Christian Religion*, ed. John T. McNeil, vol. 1 (Lousville: Westminster John Knox, 1960), 35-38.

3. Invite other people into your life.

You're going to have days when you forget. You're going to have seasons when you lose sight of God and fail to meditate on the gospel. God knows this, and it's one of the reasons he has given us the wonderful gift of the church. God wants us to be connected with other believers in a local body so that we can feed off of each other. You need other people in your life who will tell you when you're moving away from Christ. The local church is where God intends for you to find those relationships.

4. Guard your heart against the world.

The world stands in opposition to the gospel. Satan desires to oppose God's kingdom at every turn. If you listen uncritically to the messages embedded within culture, you will be swayed. The world tells us to live for ourselves, to build our own legacies, to follow our dreams. All of these messages have one premise in common: Your identity is up to you. Build yourself up, because no one else will. That is an obvious lie. God builds us up in Christ. We need to be aware of the subtle ways in which the world preaches a different gospel.

Living Free

Imagine a debate between Miley Cyrus and Bob Dylan. I know, I know, that seems far-fetched, and sadly some of you reading this won't even know who Bob Dylan is. But bear with me, because he's been on the stage for 50 years and Cyrus will likely be irrelevant by the time you finish reading this paragraph. For many, Miley Cyrus epitomizes the prevailing notion of what it means to live the good life. She's rich and she's famous, and she doesn't care what anyone else thinks. She's living life her way, and that's the ideal so many of us strive after. In the words of Cyrus, "It's our party we can do what we want…we can say what we want…we can love who we want…we can kiss who we want…we can sing what we want." What we want defines us, and we certainly don't want anyone else telling us what to do. Children can't wait to get out of the house so that they no longer have parental restraints. College students fantasize about being the boss so that they don't have to answer to anyone else. No one likes the police, because, let's face it, they exist to ruin everyone's fun. Freedom in life, and happiness, is achieved when we can do what we want, when we want.

Enter Bob Dylan and these timeless lyrics: "It may be the Devil or it may be the Lord, but you're gonna have to serve somebody." Yes indeed. Dylan doesn't believe that Cyrus' definition of freedom and happiness is possible. He's calling her celebration of "freedom" baloney. In other words Dylan doesn't believe that anyone lives his or her life without being a slave to someone or something. And Dylan's right. The apostle Paul sides with Bob Dylan in this imaginary debate: "Do you not know that if you present yourselves to anyone as obedient slaves, you are slaves of the one whom you obey, either of sin, which leads to death, or of obedience, which leads to righteousness" (Rom. 6:16)? The issue for Paul is not whether we are slaves, but to whom we are slaves.

No one is free from slavery. That may sound controversial to you, and you may be looking for some proof texts to contradict what I'm saying. After all, doesn't the gospel say we are free? Let's try John 8:36: "So if the Son sets you free, you will be free indeed." Jesus is talking about freedom, but he doesn't define it quite like Cyrus does. The freedom of the cross is freedom from one kind of slavery (to sin) toward another kind of slavery (to God/Christ/righteousness). In fact, freedom from sin is what John 8:36 is all about. Miley Cyrus may think that she's free, and you may think she's singing about something you want. But the Bible says that's not freedom at all. For a sinful human being to do whatever he or she wants is the very definition of slavery. It's slavery to sin, and it leads to death.

The gospel frees us to live as slaves to God instead of slaves to sin. This is not possible without Christ's work on the cross and in his resurrection. Rom. 8:8 says, "Those who are in the flesh cannot please God." We were created to live for God's glory in obedience and love. Ever since Adam, we have all failed to live lives true to our calling. We have opted instead to go our own way, thinking we were choosing freedom. As a result of our rebellion we have enslaved ourselves to sin. We have merely exchanged one master (God) for another master (sin). But just as God raised up Moses to set his people free from slavery in Egypt, he has also raised up Christ to set us free from slavery to sin. If we belong to Christ we are able, for the first time in our lives, to live in true freedom. We are able to obey God with loving and worshipping hearts, achieving the ultimate purpose for which we were created in the first place. Because of the cross and by the Spirit's enabling power, we are able to say no to sin's enslaving power and to say yes to life lived for God. To be truly free is to be a slave of Christ.

That's why the New Testament is filled with admonitions to "obey" and to "submit." Freedom is never defined in terms of unrestrained desire. Freedom is always defined by restraint and self-control. The gospel frees us to live for God, which means we will live in obedience to God's commands (Rom. 8:7; Jam. 4:7; Acts 5:32; Heb. 12:9). It also means we will recognize and submit to God-ordained authority: children to parents (1 Tim. 3:4; Eph. 6:1; Col. 3:20); church members to church leaders (Heb. 13:17; 1 Cor. 16:16; 2 Thess. 3:14; 1 Pet. 5:5); wives to husbands (Eph. 5:22-24; Col. 3:18; 1 Pet. 3:4-5); and citizens to government (Rom. 13:1; Tit. 3:1; 1 Pet. 2:13). The Christian freed from sin does not shake his fist at God-ordained authority and cry out, "I can do what I want!" Submission to authority is only possible for free people, because ultimate authority belongs to Christ (Eph. 2:22).

God Can Do Whatever He Wants

"Let us get this one thing straight," writes Virginia Stem Owens in her now famous quote that can be read all over the Internet, "God can do anything he damn well pleases, including damn well. And if it pleases him to damn, then it is done, ipso facto, well. God's activity is what it is. There isn't anything else. Without it there would be no being, including human beings presuming to judge the Creator of everything that is." Owens certainly chooses a provocative way to say it, but her words convey an important idea that we seem to have lost in our age, even among Christians. I am convinced that a biblical view of the world must begin with submission to the God who can do whatever he pleases.

Owens is advocating a proper recognition of what 19th century Danish philosopher Soren Kierkegaard once called "the infinite qualitative distinction between God and man." In other words human beings must not presume to have the ability to fully understand God and his ways. We can know God truly, because God reveals himself, supremely so in Jesus Christ. However, we can never know God exhaustively, nor fully come to understand why he does what he does beyond what he has told us. Thus, it would be foolish for sinful, finite man to ever suppose that he is an adequate judge over the holy, infinite Creator of the universe. When we lose this distinction,

Kierkegaard maintained, we make a mockery of God. In actuality, God is replaced by the creature, and what is created is exalted over the Creator. This is the height of biblical idolatry.

"That's not fair." "How could God punish people forever?" "Why do bad things happen to good people?" "What about those who have never heard the gospel?" Each one of these statements could simply be honest questions from honest seekers. However, often these questions express hearts in which the infinite qualitative distinction between God and man has been abolished. He must answer to us. He must explain his ways to us. He must abide by our notions of fairness. And against this foolish murmuring the Bible says unashamedly: "Our God is in the heavens; he does all that he pleases" (Ps. 115:3). For the heart submitted to God's lordship in Christ and shaped by the Bible, this presumption sounds crazy. Isaiah accuses people who have this desire to judge God of "turn[ing] things upside down," and goes on to ask, "Shall the potter be regarded as the clay, that the thing made should say of its maker, 'He did not make me'; or the thing formed say of him who formed it, 'He has no understanding'?" (Is. 29:16).

The greatest evidence that we have lost the distinction between Creator and creature is found in the very questions we are asking. Notions of God's fairness are never even discussed in the Bible; they are presupposed. Of course he's fair. He defines what is fair. We don't take our own notions of fairness to him. We get our notions of fairness from him. Think about this: The problem in the biblical storyline is never, "How could bad things happen to good people?" There are no good people! The drama of Scripture answers a completely different question: "How could anything good come to these wicked rebels?" Which question is more difficult to answer for you? Be careful how you answer this, because you may be upside down in your view of God. Of course, the glorious answer to this question leads us to the person and work of Jesus Christ. Our sin is absorbed by him bearing God's wrath as our substitute and his righteousness is given to us (2 Cor. 5:17). Because of Christ we are treated with grace and love, as God's very own children, when we deserve nothing but wrath and damnation. Praise be to God!

What does this mean for Christians? It at least means that we should seek to conform our minds to God's mind as we pursue being shaped by the Scriptures concerning these things. The biblical writers are never ashamed of the doctrine of God's wrath and neither should we be. We should embrace his wrath as beautiful even as we weep for those under it. I think this is the proper perspective. God's wrath is an expression of his perfect holiness and justice. For God to not have wrath would mean that he is not God. His wrath is indispensable to his nature, so much so that it cost him his Son as a substitionary sacrifice in order for his love to be displayed in the salvation of sinners. Does that seem fair to you? That the only innocent person in history was punished in place of the guilty? I didn't think so. Be thankful that God's notions of fairness are not the same as ours.

Christian = Witness

To be a Christian is to be a witness. Perhaps you've been summoned to be a witness before. Possibly you've had to testify in the court of law about someone's character, or maybe you've explained what you saw at the scene of a car accident to a police officer. If you've ever had any experience with anything like this, you probably have a good idea of what a witness does. It's really quite simple: a witness tells others what he or she has seen. In the Bible the word "witness" is used in a special sense to denote someone who testifies about God. A witness is someone sent by God to bear the message from God, particularly the message concerning the Son of God and the salvation he brings to the world.

In the period of time before Christ, the prophets were the primary witnesses to God's message of salvation and judgment (Acts 10:43). However, for a period of over 400 years between Malachi and the birth of Jesus, no new prophecies were given. Then, after this long period of silence, John the Baptist arrived to bear "witness that [Jesus] is the Son of God" (John 1:34). After Jesus' death, burial, resurrection, and ascension, the apostles took up the ministry of the prophets and became the primary witnesses to Jesus' resurrection and the new way of life available to sinners through him (Acts 1:22).

Even within the Trinity this ministry of witnessing is evident. Jesus says, "I am the one who bears witness about myself, and the Father who sent me bears witness about me" (John 8:18). The Father and the Son both bear witness about the Son. Jesus is clearly the focal point of all witnessing activity. After Jesus' ascension, the Holy Spirit will get it on this ministry of witnessing: "But when the Helper comes, whom I will send to you from the Father, the Spirit of truth, who proceeds from the Father, he will bear witness about me" (John 15:26). In fact, it is the Spirit who makes the witnessing activity of the apostles possible: "But you will receive power when the Holy Spirit has come upon you, and you will be my witnesses in Jerusalem and in all Judea and Samaria, and to the end of the earth" (Acts 1:8).

The Spirit, however, is not limited to the apostles. In Acts 2:1-13 the Spirit comes down upon all the believers who were gathered at Jerusalem, and they begin to speak in tongues, bearing witness in different languages to the risen Christ. The rest of Acts describes the Spirit continuing to indwell all who repent and put their faith in Christ for salvation. To be a believer is to possess God's Spirit. To possess God's Spirit is to be equipped to bear witness about Christ to the world. The witnessing ministry of the Trinity that has come down to the prophets and apostles has now been given to the church (Eph. 2:20).

Have you ever noticed how few exhortations the New Testament gives for believers to evangelize? Don't mistake this absence of exhortation for ambivalence. The New Testament does not often exhort believers toward evangelism, because the New Testament does not recognize the possibility of believers who do not evangelize. To be a Spirit-indwelled follower of Christ is to "testify to the gospel of the grace of God" (Acts 2:24). Rev. 12:11 describes believers in Christ as conquering Satan "by the blood of the Lamb and by the word of their testimony." Our greatest weapon is our testimony about God's grace in Jesus Christ.

People who are passionate about something have a hard time not talking about it. Sports fans, people in love, art enthusiasts, and book lovers illustrate this point every day. C.S. Lewis wrote in *Reflection on the Psalms*, "I think we delight to praise what we enjoy because the praise not merely expresses but completes the enjoyment; it is its appointed consummation."[3] When you care deeply about something, it will overflow from your heart through your lips. You will talk. Are you excited about Christ? Are you passionate about the gospel? Do you speak the good news to others because it's too good to keep to yourself? Perhaps your struggles with evangelism are not problems with speaking, but problems with treasuring.

---

[3] C.S. Lewis, *Reflection on the Psalms* (San Diego: Harcourt, 1958), 95.

Why John Piper Can't be Your Mentor

I love John Piper. John Piper is one of the most brilliant Christian preachers, authors, and thinkers that I've encountered in my life. I thank God for the influence he has had, not just on me, but also on thousands of others. But John Piper is not my mentor. I try to read every book that John Piper writes. I listen to John Piper's sermons on texts or issues that I'm studying. I want to hear what John Piper has to say. But John Piper does not disciple me. Why? Because John Piper lives in Minneapolis, MN, and I live in Lexington, KY. I know who John Piper is, but John Piper has no clue that I even exist. I'm sure John Piper is a wonderful pastor; he's just not my pastor. John Piper shouldn't be the biggest influence in my life, because John Piper cannot lead me, love me, and hold me accountable. And neither can any other famous Christian leader that has no personal connection with my life.

Just to be clear: I'm all about having mentors. In fact, the Bible gives us a pattern for discipleship that we are supposed to follow. It looks like this: "What you have heard from me in the presence of many witnesses entrust to faithful men who will be able to teach others also" (1 Tim. 2:2). Paul writes to the Corinthian church something similar: "Be imitators of me, as I am of Christ" (1 Cor. 11:1). Jesus had twelve men who followed him throughout his earthly ministry. Eleven of those men (plus Paul and Matthias) became the foundation of the church, as they passed down what they learned from Jesus to new generations of Christians. These new generations passed it on to newer generations, until the gospel spread throughout the entire world. This is the way God has chosen to spread the good news of the kingdom.

But I want you to notice one thing about these biblical examples: all of these people had real relationships with one another. Those who were discipling new Christians actually knew them. They could see their flaws and their gifts. The ones being discipled had to do so under the watchful eyes of real people. There was real rebuke going on. You better believe that sometimes feelings got hurt—and that was a good thing. I know that I would not be half the man I am today if it were not for God putting two godly mentors in my life. While both of these men are heroes to me, they will never be distant celebrities. I listen respectfully to them, and submit to their guidance. I imitate them as they imitate Christ. But they've won that respect through sacrificial love and Christ-like leadership.

Truthfully, it's a lot easier to claim John Piper or some other famous Christian leader as your mentor (that is, unless you live in Minneapolis and he really is your mentor!). You can take what you like and leave the rest. You can pick him up when it's convenient and put him back down when it's not. You can hear some of his words and plug your ears to others. You don't ever have to worry about being called in for a confrontation about some blind spot in your life. You don't ever have to think about having your life critiqued or about having the spotlight shine on your most glaring character flaws.

You can live your life with John Piper's sermons on your iPod and a copy of *Desiring God* right beside your bed. And while those things are sure to help you grow, if that's all you have, you will never grow in the life-on-life, in-the-trenches-with-someone-else, way that God ordains. You may conveniently miss the pain of confrontation and rebuke, but you'll also miss the joy of being really mentored in the context of a local, loving, real-life relationship.

My advice? Find a man or a woman in your local church that you respect, and ask him or her to mentor you.[4] You may even get to recommend books to them by John Piper.

---

[4] At this point I think it's necessary to clarify that if you are young man, you should ask another man to mentor you. If you are a young woman, you should ask an older woman. While this may seem obvious to you, I did have someone ask this question once. These days, you can't take anything for granted!

Consuming the Church

Allow me to introduce you to my friend, John. John is a sophomore at the university. He's also a Christian. He was saved at an early age and comes from a Christian family. He spends most of his time away from school on mission trips. Anyone would tell you that John's a great guy. John's typical week is full of spiritual activity. He participates in one of the local campus ministry's weekly worship gatherings. He loves joining with other college students every week to worship his Lord. On the weekends he visits various churches. He really likes the worship style at one particular congregation and attends there most Sundays. It really leads him closer to God. However, the fellowship this church offers isn't really appealing to John. He just doesn't connect. He's got some good friends that are members of another church in town, and he typically joins them for their church's small group meeting on Sunday evenings. He likes being able to take the parts of these churches that fit him best, while leaving aspects he doesn't particularly like. He knows it's not an ideal scenario, but he's only got a few years left in town anyway. If one of the churches would just meet his criteria he would commit. It's not his fault they all fall short.

John is a church consumer and made-up—well sort of. I've actually met many students who are just like John. I would call John the stereotypical Christian college student. John has been culturally programmed to think like a consumer. The world offers John an ever-expanding list of choices, always trying to appeal to John's preferences, and church is really no different. Many churches appeal to this shopper mentality by marketing themselves just like other products in society, trying to appeal to the preferences of the sovereign consumer. It's really no surprise that John approaches finding a church with the same mindset as a college freshman at the school cafeteria. Take this from there and that from there and put it all together on one tray. John is custom-making his spiritual program to fit his desires. And who could really argue with John's approach? These churches and ministries are teaching truth, after all. John's parents are relieved that John has found so many spiritual activities to get involved with. It sure beats the alternatives.

But John is in great spiritual danger. John is approaching the Christian life from a mindset that asks one question: "What's in it for me?" And that's precisely the opposite perspective that Christ's followers are supposed to have. Peter lays it out for us: "As each has received a gift, use it to serve one another, as good stewards of God's varied grace" (1 Pet. 4:10). Paul explains it like this: "To each is given the manifestation of the Spirit for the common good" (1 Cor. 12:7). Trace this logic: As a result of God's grace in our lives, each Christian has received a gift from God. But this gift is not given for our own benefit. The reason God gifts each believer is so that each believer will use his or her gift to serve the church. If we fail to serve the church, we are not good stewards of God's grace. And Jesus doesn't have nice things to say about those who are not good stewards of God's grace (Matt.

25:14-30). It's extremely dangerous to misuse what God has entrusted to us.

John may think he's growing from this assortment of spiritual activity, but he's really not. We grow as we learn to love. We love as we commit our lives to other people. Love is putting aside our preferences in service to others. John is championing his preferences, and as a result the only person being loved and served is John. Dietrich Bonhoeffer warned of the dangers of John's approach to Christian community: "He who loves his dream of a community more than the Christian community itself becomes a destroyer of the latter, even though his personal intentions may be ever so honest and earnest and sacrificial…Because God has already laid the only foundation of our fellowship, because God has bound us together in one body with other Christians in Jesus Christ, long before we entered into common life with them, we enter into that common life not as demanders but as thankful recipients."[5]

Once we have found a church that champions the gospel of Jesus Christ, that preaches the Bible as the inerrant Word of God, that we agree with doctrinally— a church that pushes us out toward mission and toward accountable fellowship with one another—when we've found that church—our preferences must recede into the background. God does not allow us to divide based on preferences. In this kingdom, there is neither Jew nor Greek, slave nor free, male nor female, because "you are all one in Christ Jesus" (Gal. 3:28). We could add our own contrasts to Paul's list: neither young nor

[5] Dietrich Bonhoeffer, *Life Together* (San Fransisco: Harper, 1954), 27-28.

old, neither cool nor nerdy, neither athletes nor bookworms, neither hymn lovers nor Tomlin fans. The point is clear: our preferences must no longer rule the day. They have been replaced by the perfect preferences of a better King, and unlike us he loves diversity. We don't shop for and consume the church the same way we shop for and consume products on Amazon.com. If anything, we are called to be consumed by the church as we continually die in service to a particular group of ordinary sinners.

Ordinary Folks You Can't Live Without

Every year around August, thousands of college students take up residence in my city. A few of them are Christians. And among those Christians, a smaller few are church members. And it's always this time of year when I begin reflecting on why this disparity exists. Why do Bible-believing Christians insist that the church is unimportant? And what is it that God sees in this community of misfits that college students want no part of?

Perhaps it's the ordinariness of church. It really doesn't seem all that special. Walk into a random church on Sunday morning. What will you see? Nothing exceptional. Cheap tasting coffee. Mini-vans in the parking lot. Elderly people with comb overs and too much perfume. Children who won't shut up during the sermon. It just seems so ordinary, so underwhelming. Now compare what you see at church to what you know about college students: Hormonal. Individualistic. Hard-to-impress. Entertainment-gorged. Now here's the challenge: How do you communicate to individualistic, entertainment-seeking, hormonal college students that they not only need Christ, but they also need this group of ordinary, unimpressive misfits? It's a tough job, but Jesus doesn't present it as an option.

Here's what I know: I know that beyond the generic, "How are yous?" in the Fellowship Hall and behind the stench of soiled diapers in the nursery area,

41

there's something glorious at work. God is accomplishing his glorious purposes through ordinary people. He's choosing ordinary "clay pots" (2 Cor. 4:7), people like you and I, to display his kingdom on this earth. He didn't gather all of the world's finest people to make this happen. That's how you and I would have done it, right? We like to surround ourselves with the prettiest, the brightest, and the best. We like to be known as somebodies. But God doesn't allow somebodies to be part of this. Only nobodies (1 Cor. 1:26-31). And here's where I think many college students miss it. So many college students are still trying so hard to be somebodies, trying so hard to convince themselves that they don't need anybody. So many are lusting for something bigger, something better, something more fulfilling. But God keeps pointing us to this group of people over here—this police man and that teacher and that retiree. And he's trying to convince us that there's really something more going on, something glorious happening, right under our noses. And if you can ever get past the turn-off of ordinariness to catch a glimpse of it, you will be changed forever.

Listen to what Paul says is going on when the church gathers: "Through the church the manifold wisdom of God [is] now being made known to the rulers and authorities in the heavenly places" (Eph. 3:10). The powers of the universe are looking upon the church and seeing the display of God's infinite wisdom. How does the church of ordinariness display the glorious wisdom of God? Here's how: "This mystery is that the Gentiles are fellow heirs, members of the same body, and partakers of the promise in Christ Jesus through the gospel" (Eph. 3:6). God is doing the unthinkable when that ordinary group of nobodies gathers for worship on Sunday morning. He is uniting rich and poor, black and white, male and female, young and old, the loser and the popular. No man-made distinctions can thwart this glorious work. The gospel is uniting us all into an eternal family with God as our Father and Christ as our Brother! And ordinary people are being used to display the wisdom, love, and power of an extraordinary God. Don't get so caught up in appearances that you miss what's really happening.

The manifold wisdom of God is being displayed as diverse sinners come together into one body, united under one head—Christ Jesus. So why do so many of our churches and gatherings look so monolithic? Why do we so prefer to be around people just like us? Why do Christian college students line up to go to their campus ministries but sleep-in on Sunday mornings when the real church gathers? Why are there churches for hip people and churches for old people and churches for white people and churches for black people? Let us never be guilty of separating what God has joined together. They may be ordinary, but you and I desperately need them.

Going to Church is Too Safe

"Where do you go to church?" This is one of the first questions we ask when we meet a fellow Christian. But I was struck by the late Chuck Colson's response when asked the question by Ted Kluck, co-author of *Why We Love the Church*: "I've always resented the phrase 'Where do you go to church?' I don't go to a church; I'm a member of a church. You don't ask where somebody 'goes' to a country club. I'm not talking about where you're going. I'm talking about where you plant your flag and say, 'This is where I'm a Christian.'"[6]

Language can be very tricky. Most of us talk about "going to church" without ever raising an eyebrow. But Colson's right. Church isn't a place where you go once a week, or even several times a week. It's a community that you belong to. It's a group of flesh and blood people that you are committed to and a part of. It's a family. The book of Ephesians uses at least four images to describe the church: family (Eph. 2:19), body (Eph. 4:11-14), bride (Eph. 5:22-33), and temple (Eph. 2:20-21). All of these images imply more than a weekly event that you attend. They imply lifelong commitment, something you actually belong to. We talk about "going" to church in our context, because for too many Christians, that's all it is. We roll out of bed and

---

[6] Kevin DeYoung and Ted Kluck, *Why We Love the Church* (Chicago: Moody, 2009), 146.

passively attend a service once a week (if that) where we hear songs and listen to a sermon. Then we return home without ever really having to interact with anyone. Sadly, it's often just a box that we check off. But that's not what the church is. That's way too safe.

Reflect on this description of the first century church and compare it with your own involvement: "And they devoted themselves to the apostles' teaching and fellowship, to the breaking of bread and the prayers. And awe came upon every soul, and many wonders and signs were being done through the apostles. And all who believed were together and had all things in common. And they were selling their possessions and belongings and distributing the proceeds to all, as any had need. And day by day, attending the temple together and breaking bread in their homes, they received their food with glad and generous hearts, praising God and having favor with all people. And the Lord added to their number day by day those who were being saved" (Acts 2:42-47).

When the Bible talks about church, it's never safe. Church is dangerous because you are thrown into a group of people who aren't necessarily like you and told that now you are a family, and all those crazy people must be embraced and loved as family. You may never again rely solely on yourself in life. You need other people, and that's frightening. That requires self-crucifixion. Church doesn't allow us to remain anonymous. Family members aren't anonymous. Being a member of Christ's bride prohibits us from keeping people at arm's length. We know each other, warts and all. And, in spite of those warts, we still love each other.

We don't go to church. We are members of a church. Family members. When you're dealing with family, you don't run off when folks tick you off. You don't bail when things don't go your way. We're talking about lifelong commitment. "Do you belong to a church family here in town?" Now we're using biblical language. Jesus didn't die to purchase a meeting that takes place once a week. Jesus died to purchase a family of people, centered upon his Word, who are busy doing Kingdom work together, waiting for his return. If you feel safe at church, if you never feel threatened, you probably don't get it. You're probably just "going to church."

How to Grow Spiritually

How do you grow spiritually? It seems to be a popular question as it turns up over eight million Google search results. As I began to click some of those results, I found many expected and helpful answers: pray, read your Bible, memorize Scripture, read Christian books. My problem is not with any of these suggestions. This is all very sound and biblical advice. But I was shocked by an omission. Roughly 40% of the links I clicked on did not mention the church at all, and the 60% of the articles that did mention the local church presented it as a step alongside the other steps. How do you grow? Go to church, read the Bible, and pray.

Somehow the American church has adopted a very individualistic understanding of Christian growth. We treat it much like we treat gym membership. How do you get in shape physically? Join the gym and start working out. Watch your diet. How do you grow spiritually? Join the church and start showing up. Read your Bible and pray. At this point you're probably wondering what I'm critiquing. I'm certainly not criticizing joining a church, reading your Bible, and praying. Please do these things! You won't grow without them. My problem is the way we see growth as something we do on our own. Spiritual formation is dependent on me practicing these exercises. Church is just one of the things on my list that I must do to grow. This understanding only gets at half the truth.

Consider two passages: Acts 2:42-47 and Eph. 4:11-16. Acts 2:42-47 presents us with the earliest description of the church that formed around the apostles preaching in the first century. The description presents us with a group of people who confessed Jesus as Lord, devoted themselves to the apostles teaching, breaking bread, and prayer—normal things that churches do together. But now listen to v. 44: "And all who believed were together and had all things in common." This early church was not just a group of Christians who met once or twice a week. They did everything they did *together*. Like a new family they even shared their possessions with one another. Their praying and Bible reading weren't just personal spiritual disciplines. They were sharing these things with one another. The church wasn't a spiritual gym. It was the primary hub and center of their lives together.

While Acts 2 is descriptive of growth, Eph. 4:11-16 presents us with a theology of growth. Surprisingly, the church is central in Paul's growth model. This often overlooked passage begins with the leaders of the church, pastors and teachers, equipping the saints for the work of ministry (4:11). What is the result of this equipping? The goal is that the entire church would "all attain the unity of the faith and of the knowledge of the Son of God, to mature manhood, to the measure of the stature of the fullness of Christ" (4:13). The secret ingredient in this description is "love" (4:15, 16). As the church is equipped, we learn to love one another, and the result is spiritual growth of the whole body. We grow together.

The vision of these passages is that growth is not possible on our own. You cannot love on your own. In order to grow you must love, and God's plan for us to love comes in this body called the church. As we live out the gospel together, we grow proportionately together. This vision means that I am dependent upon others in the body for my personal growth, and others are dependent upon me. Hands don't grow out of proportion to the rest of the body. Feet are not supposed to be abnormally smaller than the body. The properly functioning body grows together, all of its parts in proportion to one another. If you really want to grow, commit your life to this group of folks called the church and start loving them.

The Idol of Convenience

How do you grow as a Christian? We all want to know the answer to this question, but I'm not sure we will all like what we find. We have been conditioned to expect things to come easily. Advertising promises us better products, apps for organizing our lives, faster results. Some predict that the average American is exposed to as many as 5000 advertisements per day. Each one of these advertisements is trying to convince us that our lives would be vastly improved if we bought the product being peddled. The worldview that inevitably results under these conditions is one that binds quality of life to material possessions. Those who possess much live well. Those who possess little live miserably. Christians know this is a lie from hell, but that doesn't mean it's a lie we're exempt from believing. As a by-product of living in a culture that defines the good life in terms of material possessions (materialism, for those who like labels), we all come to have certain expectations about our world. One of those expectations that particularly harms Christians who want to grow is the expectation that life should be convenient and trouble-free.

Growth in Christlikeness is never convenient. It can't be bought with money. It can't be accessed on a website. It can't be gained in one summer on a mission project. It's not something you can take a class for. Believe it or not, they don't make an app for Christian growth. Instead, it's intrusive and bloody, cross-shaped and self-denying. It will cost you your life. In fact, you never grow as a Christian by focusing on growing as a Christian. Growth is always presented in the Bible as the by-product of suffering in love and service to God and other people. We grow as we follow in the footsteps of Jesus. We grow by loving. Jesus explains the pattern clearly: "If anyone would come after me, let him deny himself and take up his cross daily and follow me. For whoever would save his life will lose it, but whoever loses his life for my sake will save it" (Luke 9:23-24). Consider these three passages from the New Testament:

> **Rom. 5:3-5:** "More than that, we rejoice in our sufferings, knowing that suffering produces endurance, and endurance produces character, and character produces hope, and hope does not put us to shame, because God's love has been poured into our hearts through the Holy Spirit who has been given to us."

> **Jam. 1:2-4:** "Count it all joy, my brothers, when you meet trials of various kinds, for you know that the testing of your faith produces steadfastness. And let steadfastness have its full effect, that you may be perfect and complete, lacking in nothing."

> **1 Pet. 1:6-7:** "In this you rejoice, though now for a little while, if necessary, you have been grieved by various trials, so that the tested genuineness of your faith—more precious than gold that perishes though it is tested by fire—may be found to result in praise and glory and honor at the revelation of Jesus Christ."

Paul, James, and Peter all agree. Growth is not easy. It comes through suffering. In fact, it is this reality that enables us to rejoice as we encounter trials. Do we rejoice because we are unharmed and unfazed? Do we have some twisted numbness that enables us to feel no pain when trials come our way? Are the apostles advocating Stoicism? Absolutely not! We are able to rejoice, even in our great pain, because we see the bigger picture. Behind every excruciating trial, we see unfathomable glory. Behind every inconvenience we see our Father at work shaping us and molding us. We see the finished product: conformity to Jesus Christ (Rom. 8:28-29). Christians aren't people who always take the easy way. We take the Jesus way, the same one first blazed by our Lord and Savior, knowing that this route will likely require suffering. In fact, we understand that Jesus' way is much harder than the way we would have chosen for ourselves (Matt. 7:13-14), but shortcuts aren't an option. If we try to take shortcuts, we miss out, not only on the trial, but also on the growth.

Feeling Good

Let me let you in on a little secret: Right before I preach a sermon, my stomach usually feels like it's in knots. In those moments I don't even try to eat anything. Sometimes I even feel nauseous. To put it simply, I never have what some may call "a peace" about it. Quite frankly, sometimes it feels more like a war. The same feeling comes over me right before I have to confront a brother in Christ who is living in sin. It's also the same feeling I get sometimes when I have to admit to someone that I was wrong. There are a lot of things that God's Word calls me to do that I don't feel peaceful about.

Somehow the American church has come to believe that the feeling of peace in one's heart should be the sovereign determiner of one's actions. You've heard the lingo. How do you know God's will in any situation? "Well, I've prayed about it, and God has given me such a peace." Recently, I had to confront a brother about not fulfilling a verbal commitment he made to me. He responded, "I just don't have a peace about it." Why did you divorce your husband? "I just didn't feel anything for him anymore." All it takes is a reference to how one feels and any action or lack thereof can be justified.

But what if we're wrong? What if God doesn't care nearly as much about your peace of mind as you do? What if God's plan for your life actually involves a lot of discomfort and inconvenience? Could that happen?

Consider Jesus for a moment. Do you think he always felt "a peace" about perfectly obeying the Father's will during his earthly life? Early in his ministry, we find him in the wilderness, having not eaten for forty days and forty nights. Matt. 4:1 tells us the Spirit led him "to be tempted by Satan." He was hungry and he was tired. Yet he did not sin. He knew that the salvation of the world depended on his obedience. Later in his life we find him face down in a garden, sweating drops of blood, calling out in agony to God the Father as the shadow of the cross loomed in the distance. Should he have abandoned the plan because he didn't feel "at peace" about it? I'm sure glad he didn't! Today we are saved because he chose to obey God's will rather than his own gut feelings.

What about Paul? Did he always wait for a peace before he went forward with his missionary work? See for yourself. He wrote: I have had "far greater labors, far more imprisonments, with countless beatings, and often near death. Five times I received at the hands of the Jews the forty lashes less one. Three times I was beaten with rods. Once I was stoned. Three times I was shipwrecked; a night and a day I was adrift at sea; on frequent journeys, in danger from rivers, danger from robbers, danger from my own people, danger from Gentiles, danger in the city, danger in the wilderness, danger at sea, danger from false brothers; in toil and hardship, through many a sleepless night, in hunger and thirst, often without food, in cold and exposure. And, apart from other things, there is the daily pressure on me of my anxiety for all the churches" (2 Cor. 11:23-28).

Here's the point: Don't equate faithful decision making with how you feel. Often our sin causes us to feel "a peace" about the wrong decision and agony about the right one. God has a way of calling us to do hard and difficult things, regardless of how we feel about them. The Bible is a far better guide than your gut!

Staying Safe

"Be careful!" I've heard those two words come out of my mouth more times than I can count since my wife and I began having children seven years ago. Some of my concern is justified. We've been to the emergency room for concussion symptoms and fractured skulls on more than one occasion. One of my children even shot himself in the hand with his epipen at the age of three, sending a high dose of emergency adrenaline straight into his bloodstream. These things happen. However, the longer I live, the more I become convinced that most of my worries are absurdly the result, not of actual danger lurking, but of growing up in a culture that is ridiculously obsessed with safety. There's hardly a day that goes by when I don't read about some alarming safety-centric statistic on social media. Did you know that processed foods have been linked to cancer? Did you hear about the safety recall on all those infant car seats? The flu is going around church. We better stay home so that our kids are protected from all those nasty germs! Even within my lifetime the safety consciousness of America has shifted dramatically. I used to ride on the arm rest between my grandparents in the front seat of their blue Buick. Let that sink in. When I learned how to ride a bike at six, my parents allowed me free reign through my large neighborhood streets until the street lights came on. The times, they are a'changin.

I believe there's a lot at stake with safety-obsession. If Christian parents won't let little Johnny play contact sports growing up, do you really think they're going to sign off on him spending the summer after his freshman year of college telling African tribes about Jesus? What kind of character are we breeding in our young men and women when safety is the highest ideal? One of our nation's former presidents, Teddy Roosevelt, lamented this attitude at an earlier time in our nation's history when people wanted to ban college football due its dangerous nature. Roosevelt responded to the safety hysteria of his day with these profound words: "I believe in outdoor games, and I do not mind in the least that they are rough games, or that those who take part in them are occasionally injured. I have no sympathy whatever with the overwrought sentimentality which would keep a young man in cotton-wool, and I have a hearty contempt for him if he counts a broken arm or collarbone as of serious consequence when balanced against the chance of showing that he possesses hardihood, physical address and courage."

The gospel is dangerous and it's risky. It's free of cost, but it certainly demands a lot. In fact, Jesus said it might even cost us our life (Matt. 10:28). The men we read about in the Bible, the earliest followers of Jesus, almost all died for proclaiming the truth about Christ. Jesus made sure this sacrifice would not come as a surprise to any of them. He had told them from the beginning that it would end that way. He also told them that no one would die a minute too early (Matt. 10:29). Let that sink in. The One who created everything is also completely sovereign over every detail of your life. The day and cause of your death has already been determined. Would you rather arrive at that day having lived radically for the glory of the King of the universe or by living a life of self-protection and comfort?

I want to encourage you, maybe even free you, to do dangerous things. But I don't really have the power to free you for risky living. Only God does, and he's already done that in the gospel. In Christ, our greatest enemy, the thing we fear the most, death, has lost its sting (1 Cor. 15:55). If we belong to Christ, we don't have to live in fear, wondering and worrying about what lies ahead. We can live knowing that, whatever lies ahead, whatever we're about to face, the God of the universe controls our destiny. And we know what ultimately lies ahead. The promise of resurrection life in God's eternal kingdom frees us to repeat the words of the apostle, "For to me to live is Christ, and to die is gain" (Phil. 1:21).

Am I Allowed?

I'll never forget the first party I attended as a Christian. I had been to plenty of parties before. In fact, before Christ saved me, partying was my life. When my new Christian friends in college invited me to a party, I had no problem agreeing. Why wouldn't I? Put on by people from a campus ministry at my university, I was sure it would be a lot different than the parties I was used to going to. What shocked me was that it really wasn't different at all. Underage drinking, foul language, people trying to "hook-up"—all of these things were present. For the first time in my life I was introduced to what some Christians call "Christian liberty." Christ has forgiven us, the thinking goes, and we are now free to do whatever we want. Only a Pharisee would argue otherwise.

We Christians have a tendency of always seeking to push the boundaries of what's allowed to the very limit. Whenever I do "Q & As" for students, the majority of the questions I get asked have to do with boundaries. Can I listen to this type of music? Can I watch this movie? How far can I go with my boyfriend? Can I drink alcohol? We are obsessed with getting as close as we can to sin without crossing the line. What strikes me as ironic is that the very same people who accuse others of legalism for their desire to live with holiness are the ones usually obsessed with boundaries. Obsessing over boundaries and trying to get as close as possible without crossing the line is the epitome of legalism, don't you think? I'm convinced that the gospel obliterates this way of thinking. No longer are we asking, "What am I allowed to do?" The shackles of legalism have been nailed to the cross. We are now free to ask a completely different question: "How can my life most glorify God?" We're not trying to avoid sin as much as we're trying to live completely for God. It's a subtle distinction with significant consequences for the way we approach life. In fact, it's in the context of a discussion about what's allowed that Paul wrote, "So, whether you eat or drink, or whatever you do, do all to the glory of God" (1 Cor. 10:31). As you can see, we've got different concerns now.

So how does this change of perspective affect the way we approach the practical issues of what we should or shouldn't do in life? I don't have a list of rules, but I think the following concerns should guide us:

When it comes to art (movie, book, music, website), ask: Does this make sin look normal? A good story is going to depict sin. That's because we're all sinners, and sin is a part of life. If the depiction of sin in a story is not allowed, then we must start ripping pages out of our Bibles. The issue is not that sin is depicted, but the way that sin is depicted. C.S. Lewis writes fiction about sin. Lil Wayne raps about sin. There is a big difference in the way these two wordsmiths approach the topic. Lil Wayne normalizes sin. He talks as though rebellion against God is the way to success and happiness. C.S. Lewis shows the effects of sin.

In his stories he shows how sin leads to death and misery.

Can I thank God for this art form? I watch a lot of baseball. I thank God for the game of baseball. I truly believe it is a gift. Likewise, there are musicians, some who are not Christians, who I thank God for. I realize that God is the one who has gifted them, whether they acknowledge it or not. These cultural forms should lead me, however imperfectly, back to the Creator who epitomizes creativity. However, there are some things that my conscious will not allow me to watch or listen to while also thanking God.

Is it helpful? This is the question Paul is asking in 1 Cor. 10:23. He quotes a common statement and then responds: "'All things are lawful,' but not all things are helpful." Here is where Christians must move beyond the issue of what is allowed. We're not trying to toe the line between what's right and wrong. We're trying to grow in Christ and glorify God. Some things are allowable, but not helpful. While I enjoy baseball very much, it wouldn't be helpful for me, as a father and a husband, to neglect my family while I watch a baseball game 162 times a year. Does it help me grow or does it hinder my growth? Does it cause me to become obsessed with something besides God? Does it pull me away from more important things for long periods of time? Do I find my heart seeking to prize this more than I prize Christ? This is the level at which Christians must think.

Does this build up the body of Christ? As Christians we are no longer allowed to think of ourselves as isolated individuals. We are now part of the body of Christ, which means my actions no longer affect only me. In anything I choose to do, I must consider how my decision will impact my brothers and sisters in Christ. Paul is making this point in 1 Cor. 8:13 as he discusses whether or not Christians should eat meat that has been sacrificed to idols. He concludes, "Therefore, if food makes my brother stumble, I will never eat meat, lest I make my brother stumble." A similar issue in today's culture would be alcohol. While a 21-year-old Christian may feel that it is lawful to consume alcohol in moderation, we must recognize that not every Christian feels the same way. We are obligated by the gospel to defer to our brothers and sisters anytime our perceived liberty comes into conflict with his or her conscience. The gospel always compels us to consider the concerns of others before our own.

Godly Masculinity?

"Men's ministry so often falters for this simple reason: *it's actually women's ministry for men*...Few Christians would recognize a slap on the head or name-calling as godly behavior, yet for a young man ministering to another, such methods are far more effective than notes, cards, or flowers. Bottom line: we often fail to recognize godliness cloaked in the masculine spirit."[7] The church in our context appeals more to women than men. On any given Sunday in the United States, the average church is split 61% to 39% in favor of women.[8] Why is this? Most churches offer a highly feminized version of Christianity that simply does not appeal to men. Masculine behavior is generally discouraged. Risk is underplayed and safety wins the day. The result is that the majority of men are simply not interested in church. However, it's vital to note that it's not biblical Christianity that's turning men off. It's a form of Christianity that's been neutered and sanitized.

But this isn't just a church problem; it's much bigger than that. Feminist author, Camille Paglia, argues in a recent interview that in the societal suppression of manhood we're witnessing the suicide of Western

---

[7] David Murrow, *Why Men Hate Going to Church* (Nashville: Thomas Nelson, 2005), 141-143.
[8] Ibid., 53.

civilization: "Primary-school education is a crock, basically. It's oppressive to anyone with physical energy, especially guys...They're making a toxic environment for boys. Primary education does everything in its power to turn boys into neuters...Masculinity is just becoming something that is imitated from the movies. There's nothing left. There's no room for anything manly right now."[9] When a feminist begins to lament the loss of masculinity in culture, it's time to listen!

The Bible never attempts to suppress manhood. On the contrary true masculinity is encouraged on every page: "Be watchful, stand firm in the faith, act like men, be strong. Let all that you do be done in love" (1 Cor. 16:13-14). As Paul charges Timothy to press on in the power of the gospel toward discipling faithful men, he uses three masculine metaphors: soldier, athlete, and farmer (2 Tim. 2:1-7). Our Lord and Savior Jesus Christ, the one we are to imitate (1 Cor. 11:1), shows us perfect masculinity is his very person—passivity-rejecting, responsibility-assuming, courageously-leading, eternity-investing, self-crucifying manhood. We are never commanded to get in touch with our feminine sides. We are never encouraged to suppress our aggression. Instead, we are called to bring every ounce of our manliness under subjection to Jesus Christ. Our manhood was designed by God, and he intends to use it for his glory.

Christian men, don't allow the culture to make you feel guilty for being a man. Don't believe the lie that godliness is necessarily nice and quiet. It can be. But it's also aggressive and assertive. So don't be

---

[9] "Camille Paglia: A Feminist Defense of Masculine Virtues," accessed on 1/13/14, http://online.wsj.com/news/articles/.

ashamed of the fact that you would rather sing of marching into battle behind your sovereign King than songs about being in love with Jesus. Don't be shamed into checking your manhood at the door of the church. The church needs you, just the way you are. We need your love of adventure as we lead God's people to reach the nations. We need your desire to get things done as we make important decisions about our future. We need your aggression as we seek to teach our boys to be men in a feminized world. We have to stand against the cultural tide as we show the world that the church may just be the last place on earth where men are free to be men.

Time Management

You're not as busy as you think. There, I said it. And to be perfectly honest with you, it feels really good to say it in hopes that a college student or two will read this and take it to heart. For a long time I have listened to college students complain about not having enough time to do all the things they need to do. At one time I was one of those college students. By God's grace he's allowed me to gain a little perspective since then. So I'm here to break the news. Please don't misinterpret my tone as insensitivity. I have no doubt that you really do feel too busy, and that this tension sometimes overwhelms you. I am certainly not questioning the sincerity of your lament or calling into question the length of your to-do list. I just want to tell you very simply and very lovingly: You're not as busy as you think.

Here's what I know—what I've learned—about time. Your biggest problems concerning busyness and time management aren't really management problems. A time management workshop is not going to solve all your issues. It might help, but there's more going on in this struggle. Busyness is not a time management problem, because it's a worship problem. Let me explain.

Imagine this scenario: Your favorite musician/actor/athlete/miscellaneous famous person wants to meet you tomorrow. It's his or her only available time, but it's not a convenient time for you. In fact, the invitation is right in middle of the most pressing thing you have going on that day. What do you do? Certainly, you will tell this famous person that you're too busy. Tomorrow just isn't a good day. Maybe next time! But you and I both know that's not how this story would end. There's no way you would do that! You're going to move heaven and earth to make sure you are there. This is a once-in-a-lifetime opportunity. Whatever you had scheduled is just going to have to wait. Here's the point of the hypothetical: We make time for what we treasure most.

Jesus taught something very similar about money. In Matt. 6:21 he said, after teaching on the superiority of treasures in heaven over treasures on earth, "For where your treasure is, there you heart will be also." Whatever you most treasure, whatever brings you the most joy in life, will get your devotion. If you see something as valuable, you will devote yourself to that object. If you see something as supremely pleasurable, your life will include the pursuit of that reality. This is why Jesus says, just a few verses later, "No one can serve two masters, for either he will hate the one and love the other, or he will be devoted to the one and despise the other. You cannot serve God and money" (Matt. 6:24). If Jesus is your treasure, you will be devoted to him. However, if something else is your treasure, in this case money, you will be devoted to that. He will not share the stage of your heart's devotion with anyone or anything else.

What Jesus says here about money applies equally to time. In fact, these are the two ways we most express our devotion to something. We invest time and money in what we care the most about. I think this is vitally important for busy people to realize. You will make time for what you really see as beneficial for your life. If you don't have time for true fellowship with God's people, it's because you don't see fellowship with God's people as important. Or maybe you do, but you see other things (education, video games, Netflix, sleep) as more important.

So how do we fix our time problems? It's a simple answer, but the living of it is certainly not easy. When Christ becomes our greatest treasure, we will make time for what he considers most important. When we are worshiping him alone, his desires become the only concerns that matter. The sun must be central in our solar system, or chaos will ensue. Likewise, Christ must be central to the solar system of our lives in order for us to have gospel-shaped priorities. You will make time for what you care about the most. If you don't have time for the things that Christ calls you to do, what does that say about your heart? What does that say about what you treasure?

Never Again!

Have you ever told yourself, "Never again!"? Have you ever vowed to never again repeat a mistake, only to find yourself in the very same predicament over and over? Sin has a way of bringing us to make these grand pronouncements. We rebel against God, and then guilt overtakes our souls. In frustration and remorse, we beg God for mercy. We pray Psalm 51—for real this time. We repeat Rom. 8:1 over and over again in an effort to find comfort: "There is therefore no condemnation for those who are in Christ Jesus. There is therefore no condemnation…" We wallow in self-pity, before picking ourselves off the ground determined to continue on. We know it's happened before, but this time we're not kidding. Never again.

If this pattern continues for any length of time, we will begin to question some things. Maybe I'm not a Christian. Maybe it's not my fault. What if my circumstances were different? Is God doing this to me? The searching for causes can take us down some pretty dark paths. The frustration of feeling powerless in the face of a powerful enemy begins to take a toll. We grow weary. We grow cynical. We drift away from God, and the gospel ceases to delight us. We feel poor, broken, powerless, hopeless, and enslaved. We live out our days in complacency, submitted to the fact that things will never be different. Sin will always control us. We've tried everything, and nothing ever changes. Change just doesn't seem possible.

Perhaps what I've described above describes you in your battle against sin. Perhaps it's pornography. Perhaps it's an eating disorder. Maybe it's an impure relationship with a longtime boyfriend or girlfriend. Whatever it is, wherever you may be in the process, the gospel has some astonishing things to say to you. You may feel defeated, but the victory has already been won. You may feel poor, but in reality you are filthy rich. You may feel hopeless, but in Christ, you have every reason to hope. Transformation isn't just possible; it's certain. The battlefield, if you are in this predicament, is in your heart and in your mind. Your past failures and frustrations have led you to doubt some very important realities—realities that are essential to believe in order for you to change.

Consider this: "We know that our old self was crucified with him in order that the body of sin might be brought to nothing, so that we would no longer be enslaved to sin" (Rom. 6:6). Note that Paul is speaking in the past tense. These twin realities of our sin being brought to nothing and our slavery to sin having ended have already happened. When Jesus died he was bringing the power of sin to an end. He was making it possible for his redeemed people, formerly depraved, to obey him. But notice what Paul says a little later: "So you also must consider yourselves dead to sin and alive to God in Christ Jesus" (Rom. 6:11). It has already happened in Christ, but it is vital that you believe it now. The end of sin's dominion in a person's life is only accessed through faith. You must believe the truth in order to own the truth. The power of the gospel is actualized through God's people trusting in the power of the gospel. If you are going to change, your initial battle lies right here. You must believe the gospel anew, particularly its power to change you.

Peter puts it like this: "His divine power has granted to us all things that pertain to life and godliness, through the knowledge of him who called us to his own glory and excellence" (2 Pet. 1:3). All things that pertain to life and godliness? That's right, as believers in Christ, God has given us everything we need to live godly lives. We lack absolutely nothing. The gospel has made us spiritually filthy rich—Bill Gates rich. We are overflowing in resources. We are able, through Christ, to live for God's glory every single day of our lives. We never have to give in to sin again. Isn't that good news? Doesn't that make you want to celebrate? If you feel battered and bruised by sin's barrage on your soul, you now have discovered a remedy that you always had.

I am not saying that you will never sin again. Unfortunately, this present age between the already and not yet of God's kingdom, does not present us with the possibility of perfection. However, as you battle with those sins that enslave, you should have confidence that true repentance and true change is available to you in Christ. You will have to fight for it, but the weapons for war are yours already and they guarantee victory. I have seen men enslaved to pornography for fifteen years transformed by the all-satisfying Savior to never look at it again. I have seen women with eating disorders find victory through the Bread of Life. The gospel is true and it is powerful. In Christ, you really can say, "Never again."

A Plea for Thicker Skin

Christians tend to be sensitive people. Our radars are always raised to pick up any semblance of cultural disapproval. The perpetual mood on my Facebook news feed among my Christian brothers and sisters is typically one of moral outrage. Can you believe the Grammy's? How could the government be so stupid? Why are we so persecuted in this country? Some of the things I read are accurate. It certainly seems as if we live in a world where every way of life is tolerated except the way of following Christ. While I sense exaggeration frequently among my brothers and sisters, I'm certainly not suggesting that these sentiments have no basis in reality. Christians are not typically well-received, and we never have been. So I'd like to make four observations that I hope will put our current situation in perspective.

We should expect to be persecuted. Listen to the logic of Jesus: "A disciple is not above his teacher, nor a servant above his master. It is enough for the disciple to be like his teacher, and the servant like his master. If they have called the master of the house Beelzebul, how much more will they malign those of his household" (Matt. 10:24-25)? Or how about this straight-forward comment from Paul: "Indeed, all who desire to live a godly life in Christ Jesus will be persecuted" (2 Tim. 3:12). This life of following Christ is not for the sensitive. It's not for the faint of heart.

Jesus told us that we would have to follow him while dragging our own cross behind us (Luke 9:23). As a matter of fact, there is not one hint in the entire Bible that suggests we should expect anything but persecution. If you love Jesus, be prepared to be hated by the world. They hated him, they hated his apostles, and they will very likely hate you.

We really have it easy. News flash: As bad as you may think you have it here, we really aren't persecuted very much. We live in a time in history when worldwide persecution of Christians is more prevalent than it has ever been at any other time in the history of the world. If you live in North Korea, Somalia, or Syria, and openly profess faith in Christ, your life will be in danger. But that's hardly the case here in the United States. We get offended if someone does not pray in Jesus' name before the Little League jamboree. We feel persecuted because we seem to be the only people left who still think homosexuality is morally wrong. But we're not getting killed for our faith here. Not even close. And it's insensitive to our brothers and sisters in the world who are losing their lives for their faith in Christ to suggest that we have it bad. We need perspective on this. The Christian heritage of our forefathers still influences the cultural mindset enough that our unpopular convictions are at least tolerated without violence. We drive to worship with our church body on Sundays openly and without threat of harm. We are blessed.

Moral outrage does not make the gospel intelligible. To be constantly outraged and offended by every perceived slight in culture is not an attitude that champions the gospel we believe and confess. Touchiness is not a fruit of the Spirit. As Christians who believe in original sin and total depravity, we should be the least surprised that our fallen world finds Jesus offensive. As believers in a sovereign God who has already won the ultimate battle through the life, death, resurrection, and ascension of Jesus Christ, we should not live in paranoid fear. Our destiny is eternally secure. Unbelievers should see faith-filled courage as we respond to persecution and mistreatment with calm trust in our God. We really shouldn't be shocked that people hate us and hate what we stand for. "For everyone who does wicked things hates the light and does not come to the light, lest his deeds should be exposed" (John 3:20). The gospel we profess reminds us that we were at one time haters of the light as well (Tit. 3:3; 1 Cor. 6:11). But the gospel is so wonderful, our God so full of grace, and our Savior's sacrifice so sufficient, that we are now completely forgiven. Our outrage does not communicate that possibility. Instead, it communicates that we are morally superior people who can't believe how wicked everyone else is. As we celebrate who we now are in Christ, let us not forget who we used to be before Christ. Let us not forget that we hated the light as well. And let us determine to love our enemies, no matter how badly we think we are being treated (Matt. 5:43-48). So don't compromise the truth about Christ, but don't be surprised that what you believe would never win votes on a ballot.

The gospel advances through suffering. No one ever truly comes to Christ for the popularity and prestige. That's not how the kingdom of God works. Paul says, "For the word of the cross is folly to those who are perishing, but to us who are being saved it is the power of God" (1 Cor. 1:18). This message comes to turn all of our notions about the world upside down.

Serving is better than being served. Being last is better than being first (Matt. 20:27-28). Wisdom is now defined by the cross instead of the crown. We never want our lives to obscure this message. As we suffer we are displaying the wisdom of the cross (1 Cor. 1:26-31). Our weakness displays the power of God (2 Cor. 4:7). Because we know that the gospel advances through suffering, we can join Paul in boasting, not about strength, but about our weakness (2 Cor. 11:30).

Liberating Prayer

How many of you like to fail? I don't see many hands up. I've never met anyone that would answer yes to that question. If people think they are guaranteed failure in an endeavor, many will choose not to even attempt it. Failure is not a pleasant experience for people who have been raised on a steady diet of positive thinking, pumped full of self-esteem, and awarded trophies for every attempt at anything in life, regardless of outcome. We expect to win. We expect to succeed in everything. If we perceive that there's a good chance of failure, we would rather not even try. Therefore, we are a part of a generation of people who feel really good about ourselves, but cower in the face of real challenges where success cannot be guaranteed. We don't attempt many hard things.

Prayer is a hard thing. When we pause to pray, we are not only wrestling against our own slothfulness and lack of faith, we are not only contending against a culture that aims to distract us at every point, we are also fighting against principalities and powers of darkness. Satan does not want us to pray. As a result, I have never once met a Christian who told me that he or she prayed enough. I have never once met a Christian who explained to me that he was satisfied with his prayer life. Prayer really is hard, but we know that God calls us to pray and that the reward far outweighs the risk. Therefore, most of us keep trying, albeit in a discouraged state of mind.

But I don't think God intends for us to live our lives in a perpetual state of guilt, distraught because we don't pray adequately. Therefore, in an effort to liberate you from unnecessary sources of guilt concerning prayer, I would like to remind you of a few wonderful things that we often forget are in the Bible.

Remember that you are praying to your Father. Have you ever been around a child talking to his loving father? Does the father usually get out a notepad to critique the things his toddler is saying? Does a loving father usually rebuke the requests that the young child makes? Of course not! And yet it is this earthly father/child relationship that Jesus tells us to look to for advice about prayer. Here's the logic Jesus uses: "If you then, who are evil, know how to give good gifts to your children, how much more will your Father who is in heaven give good things to those who ask him" (Matt. 7:11)! Jesus wants us to be bold in our asking. God doesn't want us to be in constant limbo, worried about whether or not we are praying for the right things. Just talk to your Father. He wants to hear from you. Ask, seek, and knock (Matt. 7:7), and do so boldly.

Remember that the Holy Spirit autocorrects your mistakes. I love autocorrect on my iPhone. I have really clumsy fingers and those little buttons on the touchscreen prove difficult to hit accurately. The autocorrect feature enables me to keep typing with confidence, knowing that the phone will rightly discern what I am intending to say (most of the time!). In Rom. 8:26-27 Paul explains how the Spirit provides us with something similar to autocorrect when we pray, only his corrections are always perfect: "Likewise the Spirit helps us in our weakness. For we do not know what to pray for as we ought, but the Spirit himself intercedes for us with groanings too deep for words. And he who searches hearts knows what is the mind of the Spirit, because the Spirit intercedes for the saints according to the will of God." The Spirit is praying for us as we pray our distracted, clumsy prayers. He is fixing our mistakes and offering up our prayers according to the will of God. It's OK if you don't always know what to pray for. The Spirit does, and he will not leave you on your own.

Remember that the Bible never commends lengthy prayers. I have often read books on prayer that commend certain figures in church history for their devoted prayer lives. For example, did you know that Martin Luther prayed every day for at least three hours? Now, before you start feeling bad again, let me point out that the Bible never points to the amount of time one spends in prayer as being of any significance whatsoever. In fact, the vast majority of prayers in the Bible are rather short. Jesus' model prayer (Matt. 6:9-13) contains six petitions and can be said in less than twenty seconds (I just timed myself). Right before Jesus gives us the model prayer he warns about praying like the Gentiles who "think that they will be heard for their many words" (Matt. 6:7). This is really comforting to me, because I'm a get-to-the-point type of guy. I have never enjoyed chatting on the phone or texting back-and-forth for long periods of time. Once I've said something I really don't see the need to belabor the point. And according to Jesus that's just fine! Afterall, "Your Father knows what you need before you ask him" (Matt. 6:8). God doesn't have a stopwatch out to determine if your prayer was long enough. Praise him, give him thanks, and make petitions, but don't feel bad about praying short prayers. Jesus did it too.

How to Find the Will of God

Of all the questions I've been asked in ministry by college students, questions about finding the will of God for one's life have to be near the top of the list. Who should I marry? Where should I go to church? What should be my major? What graduate school should I choose? What dress should I wear? What ministry should I be involved in? These are just some of the examples. Here's a statement that may shock you, but has the power to liberate you: God does not usually reveal the answers to these questions. There is no right answer to these questions. It is not God's intention for you to agonize over every decision you make in fear that you may make the wrong decision and forever ruin your life.

Instead of focusing on what God has not revealed, we would honor God most by seeking to live our lives by what he has revealed. He has given us his words in the Bible. In Scripture, Paul tells us, we have everything we need to "be competent, equipped for every good work" (2 Tim. 3:17). In other words you and I have enough revelation to live God-honoring lives for the glory of Jesus, no matter where we go to school or what career we choose. It's really simple. The Bible tells us how to live and it tells us how not to live. In Christ, we are graciously provided with everything we need to obey God's will. We are no longer enslaved to sin (Rom. 6:6)! "His divine power has granted to us all things that pertain to life and godliness" (2 Pet. 1:3)!

These twin truths, that God has revealed himself in such a way that we can live our lives faithfully devoted to him and that the gospel has so transformed us that we are Spirit-enabled to live our lives faithfully devoted to him, should be liberating realities. We are not lacking anything. No new revelation is needed. No new power is required. The only thing left for us to do is live for Jesus in whatever circumstances we find ourselves. Circumstances never prevent us from living for God. Instead, they provide the opportunities for our lives to glorify him in new ways. Therefore, it is possible for us to glorify him in any and every circumstance of life.

So far my response to the question may sound like a cop out. That's great, you say, but tell me if I'm supposed to marry Jim! Let me provide you with a method that I use to make decisions in life when God has not revealed a clear answer.

1. **What does the Bible say?** The Bible doesn't tell us who to marry, but it does provide enough guidance for us to make a good decision. Is the person a member of the opposite sex? Is the person a Christian? Is the person accountable to a local church and growing? Men need to ask if the woman agrees on gender roles in the home. Does she want to be led? Women need to ask if the man is capable of being a good leader, protector, and provider. The Bible tells us this much, but it really doesn't go any further. It doesn't need to. That's all we need to know. If you can answer these

questions satisfactorily, you should be able to make a God-honoring decision.

2. **What does my church say?** God does not intend for us to make big decisions alone. Thankfully, he has given us pastors and disciplers to lead us and offer wisdom when big decisions come our way. If you do not have a local church to turn to, you need to find one. You and I are not wise enough to make momentous decisions without the perspectives of godly men and women.

3. **Pray and act.** Prayer is important, but not because you're necessarily going to feel a peace about the decision. Prayer is important because it is through prayer that our hearts trust in God and submit to his leadership in all things. Don't make a decision without prayer! But once you've sought his will in his Word, talked to key leaders in your church, and prayed, it's time to act. Make a decision.

Side note: Please stop using the excuse, "Let me pray about it," in order to delay having to make a commitment. So often we hide behind spirituality when we are really either afraid of making a commitment or we think we are too busy to take on new responsibilities. If that's the case, just say, "I'm really busy and I don't want to make a commitment right now." There's honor in that answer, because it's the truth. Coopting God into the dilemma of your decision-making confuses the issue and often enables you to lay your own passivity at his feet.

Don't be Wimpy

"Don't be a wimp!" These four words summarize an approach toward life that I've tried my whole life to follow. But I'm afraid we've reached a point where being a wimp doesn't have the same negative social stigma it once had; wimpy seems to be the new normal. We've been so coddled and so pampered and so shielded from inconvenience and hardship that there's hardly anyone left who's willing to stand for truth, regardless of consequences. And whenever wimpiness replaces courage as the dominant stance among Christians, the gospel loses credibility. Jesus was not a wimp; his life epitomizes courage. If we are going to follow him, if we are truly going to hold firm to the truth of the gospel, unshielded and uncompromised, we must prepare to meet the same reaction he got. Egos will be bruised. Self-esteem will be shattered. Proud people will respond with angry emotion. I hope you're fine with that.

I often wonder what role the church is playing in this coddling culture. Have we, the church, so compromised the message of the gospel that a call to repent and believe sounds cultish? Have we so lowered the bar of expectation regarding Christian discipleship that what we have no longer even resembles the muscular, gritty Christianity of Paul and the apostles? At what point must we stop calling our experiment "Christianity"? At what point does cultural compromise turn into being ashamed of Jesus (Mark 8:38)? How much water does it take to completely abolish the taste of Jesus from the cup we're asking people to drink from? I'm afraid we are operating out of a version of Christianity that is not bold enough to condemn anyone, not gracious enough to save anyone, and not powerful enough to transform anyone.

What's the solution? I wish it was that simple. All I know is that it must start with you and me. It must begin with Spirit-inspired, gospel-initiated boldness to stand in the midst of a hurting culture and compassionately shout from the rooftops, "Jesus is Lord, and he's the only way to be saved!" We must refuse to hide the hard teachings of the Bible. We must continue to call sin "sin" and righteousness "righteousness." A Savior that we are ashamed of is not a Savior worth following. We must joyfully and publically adopt the mindset of Paul who said, "I am not ashamed of the gospel, for it is the power of God for salvation to everyone who believes, to the Jew first and also to the Greek" (Rom. 1:16).

And then, when a few people hear this call and respond with repentance and faith, we must refuse to shield them from the hard truths, the life-threatening demands. We must refuse to coddle them with a version of Christianity that allows them to continue their former life with Jesus merely tacked on. We don't prioritize self-esteem, because Christ is the only "self" worth esteeming. We do not idolize safety, because people are reached and God is glorified often at the expense of our personal well-being. Our discipleship must not be more concerned with numbers than faithfulness. Our success must not be defined as culture defines it—big numbers and a flashy facade. Popularity must take a back seat to witness. Political correctness must never come before Kingdom boldness.

I don't write these things out of some misplaced sense of bravado, nor am I pointing to myself as the exemplar of what I've just outlined. What I'm saying, and what I believe with all my heart, is that there is only one true version of Christianity. Christ Jesus only outlined one style of discipleship: "teaching them to observe all that I commanded you" (Matt. 28:20). If you and I are really going to follow Christ—if we're really going to live our lives as Christians—we're going to have to reject the wimpy, neutered version of Christianity and "contend for the faith that was once for all delivered to the saints" (Jude 3).

The Majesty of Mundane

I'd like to tell you a story. Last Tuesday, I began my day by working out and spending time with God before waking my middle son, Elias, up for school. After breakfast, I drove him to the front of his school where I dropped him off. Then, I went to my office at church, where I met with three young men that I disciple in the faith. Next, I participated in a staff meeting and staff lunch with the greatest church staff ever assembled. We planned and prayed, made fun of each other and lightheartedly argued, before skyping with one of our missionaries in Peru. I came home late in the afternoon and spent a wonderful evening with my beautiful wife and children. We ate dinner together, read the Bible together, and prayed together. I wrestled with my boys and snuggled with my wife and daughters. My wife and I gave the kids their medicine and tucked them into bed, before spending some time together— just the two of us. We ended the evening by watching one of our favorite shows, and then we fell asleep only to arise the next morning to do it all over again.

That story probably seems boring to you. Nothing special. Just a typical day. But let me add some important details. Elias is our son that we adopted from Uganda. He was a two-year-old boy without a name, a birthdate, or a family, when people from the orphanage found him alone and abandoned at a hotel. He had markings from a witch doctor on his skin. When we brought him home he was on high doses of medication to stop seizures he was having every day. There was a time when we wondered if he would ever learn basic skills like talking and getting himself dressed. We've watched him mature into a typical little six-year-old boy who talks our ears off and gets himself dressed every morning. He now has a name, a birthdate, and a family. He now has a story. He's a McCall.

The three men I disciple were at one time dead in their trespasses and sins. They were enslaved to sin and children of wrath. I used to be like that as well. We were all without a name, without a birthdate, without a family. "But God, being rich in mercy, because of the great love with which he loved us, even when we were dead in our trespasses, made us alive together with Christ" (Eph. 2:4-5). We now have a name—sons of God in Christ. We now have spiritual birthdates. We are now members of the family of God that fellowships locally in Lexington, Kentucky. In God's wise providence he brought our diverse stories together. Our lives are intertwined by his design. There are no accidents in this story.

That church staff I mentioned comes from at least seven different states. We are radically different from one another. If college football fandom is a good indicator of diversity, we have it all: Auburn Tigers, Alabama Crimson Tide, Tennessee Vols, Ohio State Buckeyes, Florida Gators, Florida State Seminoles, Georgia Bulldogs, and Kentucky Wildcats. We have outdoorsmen and baseball fanatics, woodworkers and bookworms. Our interests and backgrounds are diverse, but our passion is the same: We desire to spread a passion for the supremacy of Christ in all things for the joy of all peoples. How did that happen? How did so many different personalities end up on the same team at this particular time and place in history? Miracle. God is writing this story.

That missionary to Peru? He was a college senior two years ago with the whole world in front of him. He could have begun his career and pursued marriage. Instead, he chose to take the gospel to an unreached people group in an obscure village 10,000 feet up in the Andes Mountains. He graduated from college and immediately stepped on a plane to commit the next two years of his life to serving the crucified and resurrected King of the universe. What makes a man die to his ambitions and sacrifice so much? "For the love of Christ controls us, because we have concluded this: that one has died for all, therefore all have died; and he died for all, that those who live might no longer live for themselves but for him who for their sake died and was raised" (2 Cor. 5:14-15). He realizes that he's not the author of his story.

My family is another miracle. I can remember the birth of each one of my three biological children: Josiah Garrett, Lillian Joy, and Samuel Judson. I remember vividly the first time my wife and I saw pictures of the two children who would eventually become our son and daughter, Elias Owen McCall and Eden Hope McCall. Two stories from another continent and another ethnicity are now forever joined to five stories from Lexington, Kentucky. Our seven stories have merged into one. Those three rowdy wrestlers and three sweet snugglers are part of an unfolding drama that the Author of life is writing as we speak. We live in his prose. Our destiny is in his omnipotent hands. We rejoice in that.

My wife was eighteen when she married me. She had just graduated from high school and I was twenty-four and in seminary. When we first met she was fifteen and I was twenty-one. I had no idea at that point in time that she would eventually become my wife. Her mother did. The first time her mother saw me, she told my father-in-law that I was going to one day be their son-in-law. I'm thrilled that her prophecy came true. There's no one else I could imagine sharing this journey with. My wife perfectly complements me. I love her more and more every day. The Author is good at his craft.

This story I'm sharing is nothing special. It's just an ordinary day in an ordinary life. But I hope you can see that there is far more going on beneath the surface of things. Majesty is all around us, all the time. It takes a little bit of effort—a little bit of faith-filled imagination—but the glory is always there, hidden beneath the exterior of an ordinary life. Sometimes we don't recognize it because we're too busy checking our watches, waiting for the weekend, and saving our vacation days. Sometimes Martha wins the day when Mary is needed (Luke 10:38-42). But each new ordinary day, majesty is there for the taking. Every day the Creator invites us to taste his glory. Every day we are handed a script and told to act our part in a divine drama that encompasses all of human history—a story that features the mundane just as much as the spectacular. We're not the star of this story—that part was given to Jesus. But we are privileged to get to play supporting roles. Will you spend your life looking forward to the next big thing or will you choose to embrace   the   majesty   of   the   mundane?

Why G-Rated is Dangerous

They tell us that the average American will spend around nine years of his or her life watching television. On average, that's about 2.8 hours per day, supposing that he or she lives 75 years.[10] That's a lot of time. That's close to 1/8 of your life. Whether you fall below that average or exceed it, the point is the same: Most of us spend a considerable portion of our lives being entertained by the tube. Let's not even begin to think about the Internet!

When it comes to watching television and movies, Christians like to rely heavily on the rating system. Profanity, violence, and sex are bad. Movies and shows that avoid these themes are suitable for watching, the thinking goes. It is not my intention to enter into that debate here. My point is simply that what a movie or show is rated may not be the most telling aspect of its content. There's something else going on when we sit down to watch a show that is much more subtle. Theologian G.K. Beale explains it this way:

> What is the typical TV worldview? It is a worldview with little to no awareness of, or

---

[10] "American Time Use Survey – 2012 Results," Bureau of Labor Statistics, accessed February 27, 2014, http://www.bls.gov/news.release/pdf/atus.pdf.

sensitivity to, God's working in everyday life, in the details of our life. Have you ever heard a TV character say, "Well, let's look at Scripture and see what God says about this? Let's pray about this?"...This absence of God in mainstream media should alert us to the fact that when we uncritically leave ourselves open to the perspective of the media's worldview, then, slowly but surely, it leads us to cease thinking of the things of the Lord in the details of our everyday life. In this worldview, God is not active in the specific affairs of the world or in our individual lives. *And when we imbibe this worldview uncritically, it makes us feel a little bit abnormal, a little bit unnatural in relating to God and being sensitive to his sovereign activity in our daily life* (emphasis mine).[11]

I don't know about you, but I've felt that abnormality in my heart. I've sensed the awkwardness that comes when I try to mention God in a college class or in the workplace. I've even felt weird dropping God's name in conversation with Christians. Media doesn't have to be profanity-laden and full of pornographic images to be dangerous. There's something far more subtle going on when we watch something: a worldview is being propagated. Beale is pointing out that when we absorb entertainment that leaves God out uncritically, it begins to feel natural for us to leave God out of our lives. The danger in so much of our entertainment is not necessarily what is said, but

---

[11] G.K. Beale, *We Become What We Worship: A Biblical Theology of Idolatry* (Downers Grove: IVP Academic, 2008), 299.

what is left unsaid. This danger is amplified by the fact that we don't notice it. We grow accustomed, through the hours and hours of being gripped by secular media, of thinking about life minus God. Perhaps the influence of media is a primary cause of the practical atheism that is so prevalent in our day and age.

The title of Beale's book explains this dynamic in biblical terms: "We Become What We Worship." As we devote our hearts to things, we are being changed. This can be a positive thing: "And we all, with unveiled face, beholding the glory of the Lord, are being transformed into the same image from one degree of glory to another. For this comes from the Lord who is the Spirit" (2 Cor. 3:18). However, it can also be detrimental to our souls: "Those who make [idols] become like them; so do all who trust in them" (Ps. 115:8). The question isn't whether or not you are being changed by worship. You are. The question concerns what you are being changed into by your worship. G-Ratings aren't necessarily a good predictor of that.

Why Are You So Distracted?

Have you ever sat down at your desk to work on something important only to waste countless minutes brainlessly going from website to website on your laptop or smartphone, picking up pointless tidbits of information, but never actually doing what you sat down to do? I have. We are living in a world that offers us endless possibilities for distraction twenty-four hours per day. Twitter and Facebook, Instagram and YouTube, video games and text messages, are all competing for our attention. In such a context it is sometimes tempting to despair. Even if we wanted to escape it, it doesn't really seem possible. This is the air we breathe, and for all the gifts that technology provides us, it also has consequences. As Christians, we must celebrate the benefits of technology as gifts of God, while also not remaining oblivious to some of the pitfalls of technology in a fallen world.

One of those pitfalls is our tendency toward distraction. Author Nicholas Carr writes, "What the Net seems to be doing is chipping away my capacity for concentration and contemplation. My mind now expects to take in information the way the Net distributes it: in a swiftly moving stream of particles. Once I was a scuba diver in the sea of words. Now I zip along the surface like a guy on a Jet Ski."[12] The more complicated the subject, the more difficult it becomes for us to grasp and the harder it is to focus. And herein lies our problem as Christians. We are privileged with an invitation from the Creator of the universe to enter into intimate relationship with him, to meditate on his precepts and fix our eyes on his ways (Ps. 119:15). Here we have the most complex personality in the universe calling us to take our eyes off our iPhone screens so that we can meditate on and worship him deeply. Are we even capable of such meditation?

But let's not get the wrong idea about distraction. We are not merely helpless victims in the midst of a culture of distraction. That's a false narrative. A 17th century Christian philosopher named Blaise Pascal had some interesting things to say about distraction. He saw it as a human strategy to avoid contemplating what our hearts can't bear, namely our own sin and God's infinite majesty. Douglas Groothuis summarizes Pascal's insights:

> The compulsive search for diversion is often an attempt to escape the wretchedness of life. We have great difficulty being quiet in our rooms, when the television or computer screen offers a riot of possible stimulation. Postmodern people are perpetually restless; they frequently seek solace in diversion instead of satisfaction in truth. As Pascal said, "Our nature consists in

---

[12] Nicholas Carr, "Is Google Making Us Stupid?" accessed January 5, 2014,
http://www.theatlantic.com/magazine/archive/2008/07/is-google-making-us-stupid/306868/.

movement; absolute rest is death." The postmodern condition is one of oversaturation and over-stimulation, and this caters to our propensity to divert ourselves from pursuing higher realities.[13]

The more technology grows and the digital age expands its boundaries to encapsulate more and more of our lives, the more options we have for distraction. We need to ask this question: In our use of technology, are we merely avoiding having to deal with God? What is driving us to our screens every minute of every day? Are we trying to avoid having to deal with actual reality by swapping it for virtual reality? Are we taking time each day, maybe even days each week, to purposefully put down our iPhones and contemplate the mercies of God in Christ?

---

[13] Quoted in Tony Reinke, *Lit! A Christian Guide to Reading Books* (Wheaton: Crossway, 2011), 141.

Disney Love vs. Crucified Love

"We can't be in love like the movies." At least, that's what the folk band The Avett Brothers think—something about real life being more than two hours long. I think they have a point. When my wife and I were married, I had high expectations for this thing called love. I'd watched enough movies to know how it was all supposed to work. Sparks were going to fly and we were going to live happily ever after in a state of perpetual marital bliss. At least, that's the narrative I had in mind. But the first year of our marriage ended up being the most difficult year of my life. It felt more like running through a minefield than a happily-ever-after fairy tale. I said things and did things that I will always regret.

If you buy the Disney narrative that most youngsters imbibe from an early age, love is something that comes over you. You "fall into" it, actually, much like one would fall into a hole. You are completely passive in this experience, much like having a spell cast upon you. The typical plotline usually involves an unlikely scenario of two people from different backgrounds—perhaps a princess and a beast, or a prince and a lowly stepdaughter—who end up falling in love and living happily ever after. Then the credits roll and every young girl leaves the theater fantasizing about the day her prince charming will come rescue her from her wicked stepmother. This form of love is highly emotional. The lovers usually sing about the wonder and amazement of the feelings they have for each other, and you can buy this soundtrack and listen to it at home. Every movie in this genre is a retelling of this same basic story. It has a way of burning itself into the imagination.

But what happens when Prince Charming passes gas on the night of the honeymoon? What happens when the princess wakes up the next morning with terrible breath? What about post-partum depression after the newly married couple have their first child? What about when the prince loses his job and the two can no longer pay the bills? The movies don't usually focus on these elements of the story. But you do realize that these are elements of the story, don't you? Here's the truth: those feelings of being "in love" that are so powerful do not hang around indefinitely. Sometimes you are going to feel the opposite of those feelings. Sometimes love don't feel like it should. And when that day comes and those mushy feelings are nowhere to be found, you are going to have a choice to make. You can either bail in search of a more authentic experience of love, something that 5 million Americans do every year, or you can buckle down and stick with that person because that is what you committed to do the moment you said, "I do." One of these responses is love; the other is not.

You see, Disney has it all wrong. Love is not an emotional state that sweeps a person away. The emotional element that makes us feel so good is a wonderful gift from God, but it's fleeting; it doesn't last. When that emotional bliss is missing, you better have an understanding of love that holds steady in the midst of the storm: "Love is patient and kind; love does not envy or boast; it is not arrogant or rude. It does not insist on its own way; it is not irritable or resentful; it does not rejoice at wrongdoing, but rejoices with the truth. Love bears all things, believes all things, hopes all things, endures all things" (1 Cor. 13:4-7). Love is most perfectly demonstrated in God sending his own Son to die a sacrificial death in the place of rebellious, unlovable sinners (Jn. 3:16; Rom. 5:8). The emotions of love will come and go, but the commitment of love will last forever. As you begin to think about love and marriage, focus your attention on growing as a person who loves instead of waiting for a person who will make you fall in love. I promise you won't regret that decision.

Dating Advice

Here it is—the moment you've all been reading for. Drum roll, please. The dating expert is about to lay down all of the dating advice you will ever need. I hope you sense my sarcasm. I'm not an expert, even though I should be by now. Dating is the number one topic on my counseling dial and has been for ten years. Of all the things a college student should be asking, it seems that relationships perennially top the list. There's something right about this obsession and something troubling. The first "not good" thing in God's creation was that Adam was all alone (Gen. 2:18). God's opinion on this matter hasn't changed. But, of course, God was talking about marriage, not dating. The solution to our loneliness is not a series of intimate relationships with members of the opposite sex until we find one we can spend the rest of our lives with. God's solution is one intimate relationship with one member of the opposite sex that lasts a lifetime (Gen. 2:24).

So it seems we've really messed this up. In fact, we've gotten so far off track that the biblical route now seems strange, even for Christians. As a result, Christians who desire to change the way they think about relationships and marriage often have no place to turn for help. There seems to be no one doing it differently! Others wonder what the big deal is. The Bible doesn't explicitly condemn "dating," they say. We all have to admit that there's not a clear-cut method laid out in Scripture for what a pre-marriage relationship is supposed to look like. Nevertheless, the Bible tells us some things that should guide our thoughts here: sexual immorality is sin (Matt. 5:28) and sexual intimacy is reserved for marriage exclusively (Heb. 13:4). We can also use wisdom to conclude some other things: the closer two individuals grow in relational intimacy, the more likely it becomes that they will desire and achieve physical intimacy. When this happens outside of marriage, it is always sin.

What does modern dating do? We take two hormonal people who are intensely attracted to one another, and we say, "Spend lots of time together to see if you should get married, but don't touch!" It's like telling a hungry dog not to touch the rib eye steak that's been placed in front of him. Our current system recommends acting like you're married before you really are married as a trial run. It's foolish for Christians to think that you can act like you're married in all ways except one. There are very few people that I've met who have the self-control to date for years without committing sexual sin (I continue to verify this statement as I continue to provide premarital counseling to couples). So we seem to have three options for folks who want to arrive at marriage in a Christ-honoring way: skip dating altogether and jump right into marriage, keep trying to do dating the world's way and rely on your self-control, or figure out a way to do dating that's more conducive to following Christ's commands. I don't recommend the first option unless you have extremely unique circumstances and the second option seems unachievable. So let's go with option 3.

What would it look like to date in a biblically-sensitive, Christ-exalting way? How can two people maximize the experience of marital sexual joy by not tasting it before the appointed time? I've come up with an acronym that encapsulates my advice on this subject. First, I believe that the Bible teaches that Christians should only marry Christians, and that men should marry women and vice versa (Marriage, by definition, is between a man and a woman). After these things have been established, I believe that dating should be PAPAL: purposeful, authorized, paced, accountable, and limited. Let me explain:

Purposeful. The purpose of dating must be marriage. I told my wife when we were dating, on a regular basis, "If you can't imagine me as a husband, please end this relationship." A husband is called to lovingly lead (Eph. 5:25-33), protect, and provide for his wife. Women, is the man you're dating a leader? Is he capable of protecting you and providing for you? Does he have a job and a plan? A wife is called to respectfully follow her husband (Eph. 5:22-24), helping him as he leads the family toward God (Gen. 2:18). Men, is the woman you're dating willing to follow you? Will she make a good helper? Men and women, does your potential spouse view children as a blessing and not as an inconvenience (Ps. 127)? These are the types of questions you should be asking as you seek to find a spouse.

Authorized. Because dating is purposeful and aims at marriage, I encourage men to ask the woman's father for permission to begin such a relationship. You're not asking to marry, but to begin a relationship with the goal of marriage. This step defers to the woman's father, and invites the woman's family to have a voice in the proceedings.

Paced. If marriage is the goal, you need to figure out a realistic time table for it to occur. When could you conceivably get married? If you are looking at a period of years, I recommend waiting on the relationship. Whatever your timeline, your dating should be paced so that relational intimacy should remain at a healthy level over the entire course of the premarital relationship. Our initial instinct when we find someone we care deeply about is to jump right in and begin spending every waking moment with that person. We must fight this urge. That type of commitment is reserved for people who are married. We must save not only physical intimacy, but also other types of intimacy for marriage. Find a pace that will safely bring you to the destination, should you get there at all. If you don't end up at the destination of marriage, your slow pace will ensure that you did not cross any inappropriate lines.

Accountable. You need people in your life who are asking you tough questions. For some, the woman's parents can provide this accountability. However, for many, the parents are not in the picture for whatever reason. Find an older married couple in your church and ask them to hold you accountable. Share your boundaries with them and ask them to hold you to them. Confide in respected friends and seek advice from them. Give them permission to speak their concerns as they arise.

Limited. As a general rule, two unmarried people do not need to spend time together alone in a context where sexual intimacy could occur. Couples should limit their exposure to one another by formulating wise boundaries. Remember: you are not married. What measures could you put in place to ensure that you do not act like you are married when you are not? How much time should you spend together each week? How many nights should you go on dates? How often should you text and talk on the phone? All of these things should be considered.

More Dating Advice

My wife and I were married the summer after she graduated from high school. I was twenty-four. People thought we were crazy, especially her. Didn't she want to enjoy life before getting tied down in marriage? What about a career? I find such sentiments grossly unbiblical. Marriage is not a ball-and-chain. The only thing marriage limits is our capacity to be enslaved by selfishness. C.S. Lewis explains:

> To love at all is to be vulnerable. Love anything and your heart will be wrung and possibly broken. If you want to make sure of keeping it intact you must give it to no one, not even an animal. Wrap it carefully round with hobbies and little luxuries; avoid all entanglements. Lock it up safe in the casket or coffin of your selfishness. But in that casket, safe, dark, motionless, airless, it will change. It will not be broken; it will become unbreakable, impenetrable, irredeemable. To love is to be vulnerable.[14]

According to Lewis, love is a risk worth taking, and according to Eph. 5:32 marriage is the ultimate human expression of love, displaying the mystery of the universe, Christ's love for his bride, the church. Because God so tightly unites marriage to the gospel,

---

[14] C.S. Lewis, *The Four Loves* (San Diego: Harcourt, 1960), 121.

cultural disparagements of marriage are really veiled attacks on the gospel itself. As followers of Christ, we must champion marriage as a good gift from God and work hard to accurately depict Christ's love for the church and the church's response to Christ through this one-flesh union. With marriage's importance established, here's some further advice for those who are thinking about dating.

Some of you have no business getting married right now. If you are a man who has no means of providing for a family and no future plans, you should not be getting married. If you are enslaved to certain sins, it would be best to not bring that rebellion into a marriage covenant. If you know that you are lacking in the maturity it would take to be a good husband or wife, you need to hold off. But let me be clear: marriage isn't the only thing you should hold off on; you also shouldn't be dating. Your focus should instead be on finding an older man or woman to disciple you toward growth in these areas of immaturity.

Some of you have no business waiting another second to get married. If you have been in a relationship for quite some time and you know that you are going to marry the man or woman, what are you waiting for? The notion that you have to achieve a certain level of wealth or finish a degree is not a priority that is found in the Bible. The longer you wait, the more your relationship is going to resemble marriage without being marriage. This scenario does not honor Christ. Why not go ahead and covenantally commit yourself for the rest of your life to this person you love? There will always be circumstances to justify the delay of any commitment. There's rarely a most convenient time for anything. If marriage is a wonderful gift from God that pictures the gospel before a watching world and you already know who you want to marry, it simply doesn't make sense to delay the inevitable. Men, if you want to honor your future wife and gain her trust, you will do whatever it takes to put yourselves in a position to make her your wife. What better way to earn her respect and trust and to show her your love than by working hard to make marriage a reality?

Some of you have no business remaining together at all. Over the years I have encountered many couples who remain in relationships even though at least one of them readily admits that they are not good for one another. I've met women who do not trust the men they are dating, but remain in the relationship because it provides them with a level of security. Many times, this dynamic is accompanied by a foolish hope that the other person will change in time. The gospel certainly has the power to change anyone, but that doesn't mean you should date them while it's happening. If you don't see in the person you are dating a future husband or wife, you should end it now. Marital commitment is lifelong and unconditional. Your chance to get out of the relationship is now.

Some of you have no business getting married...ever. In rare cases God calls men and women to a life of celibacy. This call is for the purpose of lifelong gospel ministry, usually in a setting that is dangerous and requires single-minded devotion. The Bible does not teach at length about this calling, but Paul possessed it and called it a "gift from God" (1 Cor. 7:7). It seems to be a rare gift that God awards to certain people in order to enable them to put undivided focus on Christ and gospel ministry (1 Cor. 7:32-35). If you desire marriage intensely, it is safe to assume you have not been given this gift. However, if you think you have this gift, talk to your church and other mature Christians in your life. Let them know, and with their assistance begin developing a plan to maximize the gift you have been given in service to Christ.

Real Dating Tips for Real Men

My two daughters are only six and five years old, respectively. However, I already get scared when I think about the potential of them getting married. It's not my fear of losing them that has me anxious. It's my fear of passing them off to husbands who are trustworthy enough to lead, protect, and provide. Here's the truth: I would not allow 95% of the Christian college men I have met in ministry to marry one of my daughters. As harsh as this may sound, I don't believe my standards are even unrealistically high. What would it take for a lucky man to receive the hand of one of my daughters? I'm looking for a man who exhibits faith in Christ, direction and purpose in life, ability to obtain and keep a job, fruits of the Spirit, leadership, and courage enough to protect from harm's way.

However, many of the young men I talk to act as if they have nothing to work on in this area. I honestly think men expect for a trophy wife to fall into their hands with the same amount of effort that it takes to obtain an Upward participation trophy. We have such a self-centered understanding of love and relationships that we focus the majority of our attention on the shortcomings of the potential spouse and very little on becoming a better husband. However, the direction of love, biblically defined, moves us in the opposite direction. Love is not about receiving, but giving. "For God so loved the world that he gave…" (John 3:16). If you want to find a godly wife, focus on becoming the type of man a godly woman would be attracted to. Here are a few practical suggestions:

Follow a Real Savior. John Calvin once wrote that our hearts are idol factories. He meant that sinful human beings like you and I are constantly looking for substitute saviors in which to put our trust. For the college student, the options are many: sex, alcohol, drugs, social prominence, sports, image, and money are all common. All of these things make promises to us that they simply cannot fulfill. We pursue these things from a universal human desire for lasting happiness, but it's an empty pursuit. As long as we pursue these things—anything—thinking that they will ultimately provide the salvation that we so long for, we will continue to exist in a perpetual state of existential misery. There's only one Savior, and his name is Jesus. He saves by dying in our place. His death wins us forgiveness, and his resurrection guarantees us abundant and eternal life. A good husband has only one Savior.

Fight Real Battles. We were created in the image of God. This reality has many implications, but one of them is the cultural mandate that we are to image God by being fruitful and multiplying, and by taking dominion over our surroundings (Gen. 1:28). God has called us to dominate our environment by bringing it into submission to him. We see Adam following this call in Gen. 2:15 as he works and keeps the garden. Work is a good thing. We were not created to be dominated by our environment. We were not created to sit passively on the couch for hours on end, mindlessly flipping channels on the flat screen. We certainly were not created to substitute real dominion with fantasy dominion by getting our dominion-taking fix through hours of World of Warcraft. If you want a woman to respect you and desire you for her husband, put the game controller down, turn off the TV, and get a job. Set some goals, and get to work on a plan to become a dominion-taking provider that a godly woman would want leading her. Before you pursue a relationship, you should at least be able to tell a young woman's father what you want to be when you grow up and be on your way toward that goal.

Prepare to Love a Real Woman. Pornography is an epidemic in culture, but it's also rampant in the church. Some sources estimate that as many as 50% of Christian men are addicted to pornography. 68% of young men look at porn at least once per week. Pornography use is widespread, and I have no doubt that many who are reading this paragraph are neck deep in it. We need to realize that sex is a good gift of God. It was God's idea. Men and women were created with sexual urges that are supposed to find fulfillment within the context of the one-flesh union known as marriage (Gen. 2:24). However, pornography offers us a way to get the sexual pleasure divorced from the real relationship. When a man looks at pornography repeatedly, his brain begins to demand more and more just to attain the same levels of pleasure. In this way pornography functions much like a drug. The more we give in to it, the more hooked we become. The more hooked we become, the more of the drug it takes to get us off. The tragic consequences of pornography on real marriages cannot be overstated. Imagine a man who has been hooked on pornography for years on his honeymoon evening with his new bride. First, he's going to expect things from her that are not realistic. Second, he is going to have a difficult time enjoying real intimacy, because his brain has been so attuned to the artificial intimacy that pornography offers. Third, he is going to view his wife, not out of self-sacrificial love, but out of a self-serving appetite to have his own desires fulfilled. His wife will simply replace the porn stars as objects to be used for his own selfish pleasure. If you are hooked on pornography, you are not ready for marriage. Real men love their wives as Christ loved the church and gave himself up for her (Eph. 5:25).

Appendix – Recommended Reading

There are several books that I think every college student or young adult should read. These books are all Christ-centered, and many elaborate further some of the themes I have touched on.

Gospel Roots

J.I. Packer, *Knowing God*
C.J. Mahaney, *Living the Cross-Centered Life*
John Piper, *The Pleasures of God*
Sinclair Ferguson, *Children of the Living God*
Vaughan Roberts, *God's Big Picture*

Gospel Community

Dietrich Bonhoeffer, *Life Together*
Paul Tripp, *Instruments in the Redeemer's Hands*
Joshua Harris, *Stop Dating the Church*

Gospel Living

Russell Moore, *Tempted and Tried*
Randy Newman, *Questioning Evangelism*
J.I. Packer, *Evangelism and the Sovereignty of God*
Paul Miller, *The Praying Life*
John Piper, *Let the Nations be Glad!*

Gospel Relationships

Gerald Hiestand and Jay Thomas, *Sex, Dating, and Relationships*
Timothy Keller, *The Meaning of Marriage*

CPSIA information can be obtained
at www.ICGtesting.com
Printed in the USA
LVHW092251091219
639926LV00005BB/1311/P

9 781490 432830